Naples 1925

MARTIN MITTELMEIER

Naples 1925

ADORNO, BENJAMIN, AND THE SUMMER
THAT MADE CRITICAL THEORY

Translated from the German by Shelley Frisch

A MARGELLOS
WORLD REPUBLIC OF LETTERS BOOK

Yale UNIVERSITY PRESS | NEW HAVEN & LONDON

The Margellos World Republic of Letters is dedicated to making literary works from around the globe available in English through translation. It brings to the English-speaking world the work of leading poets, novelists, essayists, philosophers, and playwrights from Europe, Latin America, Africa, Asia, and the Middle East to stimulate international discourse and creative exchange.

Yale University Press books may be purchased in quantity for educational, business, or promotional use. For information, please email sales.press@yale.edu (U.S. office) or sales@yaleup.co.uk (U.K. office).

Set in Source Serif type by Motto Publishing Services.
Printed in the United States of America.

Library of Congress Control Number: 2024937383
ISBN 978-0-300-25930-8 (hardcover : alk. paper)

A catalogue record for this book is available from the British Library.
This paper meets the requirements of ANSI/NISO Z39.48-1992 (Permanence of Paper).

10 9 8 7 6 5 4 3 2 1

For Ines, who led me to the crater rim

Contents

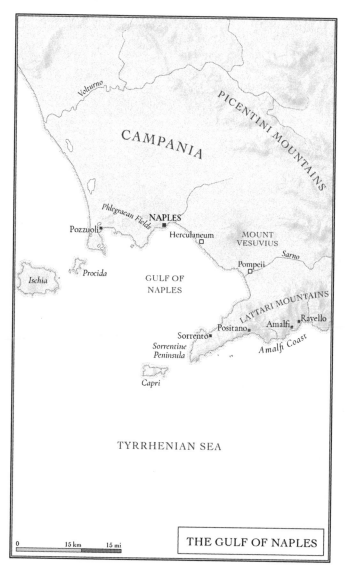

Map of the Gulf of Naples. Beehive Mapping.

Prelude

From 1924 to 1926, it was possible to dance on a volcano. You could climb down from the crater rim of Mount Vesuvius to the pit and make your way from one end to the other, through the eruption cone in the center, in about twenty minutes. In September 1925, two German travelers would not pass up the opportunity to do so. Siegfried Kracauer, a thirty-six-year-old editor at the *Frankfurter Zeitung,* and Theodor Wiesengrund-Adorno, a music composition student fourteen years Kracauer's junior, eagerly embraced this promise of the terrifying, the sublime, the unfathomable. The two men were also keen observers of the surface phenomena of their era and their surroundings. Traveling enabled them to hone their aphoristic writing skills by drawing on the quirks and oddities of the early mass tourism they encountered.

There would have been a lot to report about this at the crater rim of Vesuvius. But Adorno was not composing a satire to relate the touristic degradation of this force of nature by cable cars, souvenir stands, and idyllic postcards. Instead, he molded his impressions to form the origin and core of his philosophy. Critical Theory—one of the most powerful philosophical movements of the twentieth century and our era—came into being here in Naples, at the foot and at the crater rim of Mount Vesuvius.

The crater of Mount Vesuvius, 1925.

Naples 1925

Introduction

Theodor W. Adorno was one of the most influential European philosophers of the twentieth century. His theoretical musings on the estrangements of modernity shaped the intellectual landscape of an entire generation to a virtually unprecedented degree. He derived a new categorical imperative from Holocaust crimes against humanity and became the conscience of the intellectual reconstruction following World War II. His descriptions of right-wing radicalism in the 1960s,[1] populist ploys, and the authoritarian character read as though they were written to address the problems we are facing today.

Considering the vast scope of Adorno's life and work, one might think that there are more pressing concerns than his early travels. And even if one wanted to contemplate the influence of place on Adorno's thinking, other relevant locations spring to mind far more quickly: Vienna, the city that shaped his artistry as he studied composition with Alban Berg; Amorbach, the utopian German town of his childhood years, where he returned again and again; New York and Los Angeles, with their distinctive popular culture and a sociology grounded in empiricism, where Adorno lived during his years in emigration;[2] Paris, which he came to regard as the capital of the nineteenth century, and where he first reencountered Europe after his emigration to the United States.[3] And, of course, his birthplace, Frankfurt, where he and Max Horkheimer reopened the Institute for Social Research after the war, and the "Frankfurt School" was born.

But Naples: that sulfurous, chaotic, exhausting city? If the focus needs to be somewhere in Italy, surely it ought to be Genoa, where Adorno sometimes indulged in speculation about the noble character of his own family tree.[4] When the present book was published in Germany, there had not been a single study of the time Adorno spent in Naples. And why would there be? Adorno limited his written impressions of his journey in 1925 to a mere two letters to Alban Berg and a brief text about a Capri fisherman. Although he gathered for a "philosophical battle" with Walter Benjamin and Alfred Sohn-Rethel, who had found more comfortable arrangements in the south of Italy than Adorno and Kracauer had in Naples,[5] he claimed to have come through this battle unscathed. So why would Naples be significant for Adorno, much less for his theory?

In September 1925, when Adorno traveled to Naples with his friend Siegfried Kracauer, just before his twenty-second birthday, he encountered a colorful mix of nonconformists, egocentrics, dreamers, and revolutionaries, all cultivating a piece of the Gulf of Naples in their own unique ways. For Adorno, this turbulent panorama, imbued with a diffuse revolutionary bent, was distilled into a core group of thinkers ignited by Naples's atmosphere, where everyday life spurred even the most pensive of the participants to train their gaze on the superficial elements of their era and discern the potential in those elements. This revolutionary spark gave rise to a question: might it be possible to translate the intoxicating environment of Naples, its death cult and its exuberant vitality, into a new philosophy?

Theodor W. Adorno in 1928, and Siegfried Kracauer in 1923.

At first, Adorno seemed largely unmoved by these daz-zling possibilities. It would take years for his experience in Naples to be fully absorbed into his mind and thought. But eventually, the landscape of Naples would be transformed into the grand scheme of his philosophy. Against all odds, the clashes that arose from the philosophical battle in Naples, in conjunction with the five essays the combatants wrote about the spectacles of the Gulf of Naples, evolved into the frame-work of Adorno's thinking. The porosity that Benjamin and the Latvian theater activist Asja Lacis detected in both the rock used as a construction material and the social inter-actions of Naples became, as a constellation, the structural ideal of Adorno's texts. A southern Italian landscape that aroused a sense of longing became the source code for one of the most successful and momentous postwar theories of the Federal Republic of Germany. Naples, the apparent side entrance to Adorno's theory, leads straight into its center.

Retracing Adorno's transformation of the Neapolitan

landscape into the structuring compositional principle of his work enables us to gain a new perspective on his intellectual biography. Just as Susan Sontag's essay "Against Interpretation" argues that we should not impose a frame of interpretation on works of art, but rather unveil their essence, this book examines Adorno's texts with an eye toward illuminating the compositional logic of their arguments. Adorno had called for something quite similar as the ideal approach to music: that listeners seek to grasp a work's compositional structure instead of merely awaiting its beautiful passages. This structuring principle will turn out to be its most powerful argument, the essential instrument in combating ideology, totalitarianism, and any form of governance. It was in Naples that Adorno set forth the rubrics for this artistic approach. And his texts, which have so often led exasperated readers to declare them overly demanding, are, in the last analysis, revelatory, utterly delightful enactments of Neapolitan lunacy.

1
Island of Happiness

Kracauer and Adorno's choice of destination for their 1925 summer trip was anything but original. One of the most charming landscapes in Europe, the Gulf of Naples had been a highly popular travel idyll for decades. Mount Vesuvius is enthroned at the midpoint of a semicircle, bordered on the west by the islands of Ischia and Procida and on the east by the Sorrentine Peninsula. The aura of destruction that emanates from the volcano is a large part of the Gulf's appeal. The loose mineralized, hardened lava makes the soil unusually fertile. When the magma that has been flung farther west cools, the gases it releases render it porous and it forms a light, airy tuff: "the color of honey on the gentle, bright shores, bathed in an almost bucolic melancholy,"[1] as the Neapolitan writer Raffaele La Capria described it in 1994. "How Virgilian it all is,"[2] he exclaimed. Beginning in late antiquity, one could visit the setting of Virgil's *Aeneid,* southwest of Naples, following in the footsteps of the eponymous hero until he enters the underworld near Lake Avernus; and visit the poet's grave at the sulphurous Phlegraean Fields.

Every era creates its own havens in poetry and travel. In the nineteenth century, Naples was firmly established as the southernmost stop on the grand European educational journey. But then the painter and writer August Kopisch discovered a grotto with a mystical blue glow on a small island facing the Sorrentine Peninsula, and the island of Capri soon became the preferred destination of northern Europeans weary of civilization. The German Romantics' "blue flower" was recast as azure waters, weaving magic and allure through the entire gulf. The darker, rockier Amalfi Coast, which protects the Gulf "like a fortress from the outside,"[3] as seen from the vantage point of the Sorrentine Peninsula, would also soon be illuminated in this way.

In his 1950s essay on tourism, clearly influenced by Adorno, Hans Magnus Enzensberger describes the love of tourism as derivative of the Romantic dream of freedom. Pristine landscapes and history "have remained the models of tourism to this day. Tourism is nothing but the attempt to realize for oneself the grand dream that Romanticism projected into the distance. The more bourgeois society closed itself, the more vigorously bourgeois man sought to escape it, as a tourist."[4]

Bourgeois society closes itself off, and gives rise to the dream of an island of happiness. Secularization, industrialization, technological advancement, the catastrophe of World War I, and the subsequent failure of the revolutionary awakening led to an all-encompassing sense of crisis, a "*depletion* of the *spiritual space* surrounding us,"[5] Kracauer wrote in 1922. Referencing Max Horkheimer and others in his milieu, Rolf Wiggershaus observed, "There was a large number of sons from middle-class and upper middle-class families—often Jewish—who longed for a 'new life,' a 'new man,' and hoped to find the fulfillment of this longing in a 'new society' in which the economy did not hold sway over culture, but instead culture over the economy."[6] Back in 1914, Horkheimer had written *L'île heureuse* (The Happy Island), an impassioned prose piece drawing on elements of his own life, that listed the characteristics of the closing society: "We saw the baseness, the imperfection of civilization tailored to the masses, we had to get away from the concerns of our fellow man, away from the struggle for money and glory, away from the obligations and apprehensions, away from the wars and states, to purer, brighter spheres, to a world of clarity and true necessity."[7] Those who felt this urge to escape sought out the titular island of happiness.

Once a real island—Capri, for example—had come to embody this longing, there was no holding back. Capri was flooded with travelers from many milieus and for any number of reasons. These travelers fashioned "that idle, flirtatious life, sprinkled with hybrid crumbs of sentimentality, Central European aestheticism, and the cult of nature, which has made this island one of the magnetic points of the universe,"[8] wrote Alberto Savinio, the younger brother of the painter Giorgio de Chirico.

Adorno and Kracauer, who spent three weeks there, were only short-term guests in this setting. At the end of their stay, they met up with two acquaintances who had been lodging at the Gulf of Naples for quite a bit longer and had contributed to this heady hybrid mixture: Alfred Sohn-Rethel and Walter Benjamin.

Alfred Sohn-Rethel was in some respects a typical visitor to Capri; he could have come to southern Italy in several capacities, most obviously as a painter. The Capri landscape was an ideal source of inspiration, and many an aspiring artist with no firm sense of direction settled on painting after arriving in Capri. Alfred was born into a veritable dynasty of painters. His great-grandfather was one of the best-known German history painters of the nineteenth century; his two

Alfred Sohn-Rethel in Positano, ca. 1924, and Walter Benjamin in the 1920s.

uncles Otto and Karl, both painters, owned houses in both Capri and Positano, which Alfred frequented in the 1920s. But the family had had quite enough of painters and did everything possible to prevent Alfred from becoming one. His mother sent him to Ernst Poensgen, an industrialist and friend of the family, to ensure that he had a proper, non-artistic education. "This was a foster home, and the Poensgen household was as unartistic as could be. I played hockey and tennis there, but there wasn't a trace of music, and I was kept away from painting and drawing in this fostering framework," Sohn-Rethel later remembered.[9]

Sohn-Rethel was supposed to be going to southern Italy as an industrialist, but he made a vehement break with the industrialist career that his family had encouraged. He developed a friendship with a rebellious Russian fellow student and soon became a radical; he attended performances of Gerhart Hauptmann's naturalist plays, and he asked his mentor, Poensgen, to give him the three volumes of Marx's *Capital* as a Christmas present. He left both families, enrolled at Heidelberg University, where Emil Lederer, an Austromarxist, was teaching, and became caught up in anti-war movements under the influence of Ernst Toller. A publisher in Oldenburg offered Sohn-Rethel 250 marks a month to write a treatise on cultural philosophy; in the 1920s, it was easier to make ends meet with this sum of money in Italy than in inflation-ravaged Germany.[10] In this respect, Sohn-Rethel was part of yet another group of Capri immigrants: intellectuals in dire financial straits.

Capri provided Sohn-Rethel a locus of retreat; his work on Marx was the defense of the last bastion of societal revolution. "For all we cared, the world could come to an end, as long as Marx lived on," he wrote.[11] But then the world almost did come to an end—the revolution an ignominious failure—and Marx's theory also came under increasing pressure from bourgeois revisionism. Sohn-Rethel, refusing to stand by and watch that happen, launched the ambitious project of putting Marx's *Capital* on indestructible footing buttressed by solid scholarship. In Sohn-Rethel's analysis, *Capital* failed to live up to its own aim: when subjected to critical analysis, "none of its elements stand up to more thorough consideration."[12] And so he worked his way through the first two chapters of *Capital* in order to get them to what he regarded as their proper formulation, generating "mountains of paper" to free Marx's text from its alleged inconsistency and its persistently distracting and annoying use of metaphor.[13] Sohn-Rethel recalled shutting down communication with others in the face of his "insane level of concentration" and talking in a "near-monologue."[14]

Adorno would later describe him to Horkheimer as a

"very isolated man with a monomaniacal way of thinking
. . . who probably tries to compensate for his lack of contact
with existing things by using this sort of conceptual apparatus, just as a person who is mentally ill might attempt to up-
hold himself by invoking academic terminology and scholarly apparatus."[15] Adorno intended this characterization as
a defense.

A royal residence in an unconventional spot, a villa amid
enchanting nature: the prototype of the Capri immigrant
was the Roman emperor Tiberius, who surprised the world
by relocating the seat of his vast empire to the small island.
He is said to have attempted to leave Capri three times—in
vain—and during his final attempt, he died. At least that is
how Walter Benjamin told the story, when he noted that a
striking number of people who visit Capri "cannot bring
themselves to leave."[16] In the 1920s, Benjamin had yet to
achieve renown, but he already had a nimbus, Adorno later
recalled. At the time, readers were powerfully affected by
Benjamin's essay on Goethe's *Elective Affinities.* Just as he had
attempted to determine the "inner form" of two Hölderlin
poems in an earlier essay, he traced the truth content that
lay behind Goethe's novel and found it in a mythical element
in which the characters—though seemingly so enlightened—
are ensnared.[17]

Now Benjamin wished to examine another, incomparably more extensive aesthetic formation, and hoped that the
change of scenery would bring him the concentration he
needed to complete his postdoctoral dissertation, *The Origin of the German Tragic Drama,* in a "larger and freer environment . . . with the big picture in mind and in one fell

Capri - I Faraglioni dalla Via Krupp.

Postcard sent by Walter Benjamin in 1924 of the Via Krupp and *faraglioni* rock formations on Capri. Deutsches Literaturarchiv Marbach.

Café Hiddigeigei on Capri. Photo: Giorgio Sommer, ca. 1890.

swoop."[18] Equipped with six hundred quotations from German Baroque tragic dramas and related texts (compiled with "the best order and clarity"),[19] Benjamin set off for southern Italy in April 1924 and settled in Capri. He mused on Marie Curie's speculation that the high level of radioactivity in Capri enticed travelers into staying there; the recently discovered radioactivity was apparently considered a beneficial substance at this time. But it would not remain the only power that he felt "gathering within me—with increasing force—on this terrain."[20]

"To leave Capri without seeing the Caffè Morgano is like departing from Egypt without having seen the pyramids,"[21] Savinio wrote about the café right behind the Piazzetta, where cable passengers would alight after riding up from the harbor. This café, known as "Zum Kater Hidigeigei," gained fame as a meeting point for Capri travelers. According to Savinio it was "the most hospitable, most convivial café in the world."[22] Benjamin would concur; it was there that he met "one person after another," the "most remarkable of whom was the "Bolshevik woman from Latvia"[23] Asja Lacis, "one of the most outstanding women I have ever met."[24]

In contrast to Sohn-Rethel, Lacis came from a *successful* revolution, directly from the Theater of October in Russia. In St. Petersburg she studied revolutionary, avant-garde theater with Vsevolod Meyerhold and others, and she had established a proletarian children's theater. When she came to Capri in 1924, she had already explored the theater world in Berlin and collaborated on Bertolt Brecht's play *The Life of Edward II of England,* based on a Marlowe play about Edward II, for a production at the Kammerspiele in Munich along with her future husband, the director and dramaturge Bernhard Reich.

Lacis was staying in Capri because the climate was beneficial to her daughter's health. And of course it didn't hurt that the exiled revolutionary Maxim Gorky had established a political academy there in 1909, not far from Benjamin's first dwelling, "from which, after about four months, comrades would return to Russia with some degree of political insight."[25] (Even though this training center existed for only a few months, Capri was still the island on which Gorky could discover and admire an entirely new, human side of Lenin's character.)[26] Additionally, Lacis's theater collaborator Brecht often spent the holidays in Capri with his wife, Marianne Zoff.

After observing Lacis for two weeks, Benjamin seized his moment: he offered his help when she didn't know how to say "almonds" in Italian at a local shop. In an attempt to solidify the acquaintanceship, he further offered to carry the

Asja Lacis, ca. 1924.

almonds home. This second show of gallantry went awry: his clumsy hands dropped everything. She saw that he was an intellectual,[27] and she was unimpressed.

In the years to come, Lacis would be responsible for Benjamin's politicization, his on-again, off-again interest in communism, and his change in perspective to encompass political reality and a view to understanding the state of the world and society in the minor, everyday things that surround us.[28] Benjamin would later dedicate his *One-Way Street* to Lacis, "who as an engineer cut it through the author."[29] But now, in Capri, he was hard-pressed to respond to Lacis's tough questions about the subject he was so deeply immersed in, and what purpose his study of German tragic drama could possibly serve.[30]

Capri may have been the geographical refuge for romantics, but Naples was their social haven. Naples embodied a different, non-European world that felt almost oriental. People accustomed to a largely Protestant perspective and an industrial work culture were now presented with a juggernaut of hedonism, idleness, and lust; the phrase "savages of Europe" was bandied about. It was a paradise for anyone seeking to flee civilization. Benjamin made more than twenty trips to Naples from Capri, and with Asja Lacis, their coauthored essay (titled "Naples") characterized the chaotic multiplicity they found there. Nothing was permanently set, and everything—inside and outside, youth and old age, perversion and sanctity—could be improvised and twisted to surprising results. For Benjamin, Naples was "the most sizzling city, apart from someplace like Paris, that I have ever seen."[31]

2
Tragic Haunts

Adorno and Kracauer, like Horkheimer and the others cited by Wiggershaus, came from middle-class and upper middle-class families. Adorno's father ran a successful wine-export business, and Kracauer's father was a traveling salesman. Kracauer, like many of his generation, regarded his family's world as narrow-minded and stifling, but as an editor at the *Frankfurter Zeitung,* he emancipated himself successfully, at least on the face of it, and was established in the cultural life of the Weimar Republic, in contrast to Sohn-Rethel and Benjamin. Adorno had no need for emancipation; he consistently depicted his home life with his mother and aunt as a utopian sanctuary, and it was from them that he had his musical talent. Adorno was in the lucky position of finding his *île heureuse* right there at home. When Adorno and Kracauer headed off to Italy, they differed from those who, like Sohn-Rethel and Benjamin, stayed in the south of Italy for extended periods. They were typical bourgeois educational travelers.

So it comes as no surprise that, at first, Adorno was unimpressed by the Gulf of Naples. He wrote to his music composition teacher Alban Berg while in Capri that he was engaging in "apperception of reality here."[1] But the way he apperceived this reality was by way of mockery. Adorno wrote that "a land in which the volcanoes are institutions and the swindlers are saved" went against his public spirit; he preferred the area of South Tyrol and Vienna.[2]

The Kantian word *apperception* indicates what truly mattered to Adorno as he experienced unfamiliar places. For him, travels were not expeditions to new worlds and alternative paths in life, but merely opportunities to pursue his own theoretical interests. Later in life, he would travel in order to focus intensely on his writing during time away from academic duties, but in his early years, these were periods of enthusiastic reading. Adorno was not alone in this. After the end of World War I, on Sunday afternoons, Siegfried Kracauer had started teaching him a deliciously subversive way to read philosophical texts, using Kant's *Critique of Pure Reason*. Instead of delving into a painstaking quest to grasp a complex system, Kracauer and Adorno trained their eyes on the telling contradictions. "I am not exaggerating in the slightest when I say that I owe more to this reading than to my academic teachers. Exceptionally gifted as a pedagogue, Kracauer made Kant come alive for me. Under his guidance I experienced the work from the beginning not as mere epistemology, not as an analysis of the conditions of scientifically valid judgments, but as a kind of coded text from which the historical situation of spirit could be read, with the vague expectation that in doing so one could acquire something of truth itself,"[3] Adorno later recalled.

Traveling together was an ideal way for the pair to step up the pace of reading. Kracauer and Adorno worked their way through an impressive set of texts in the early 1920s. Nietzsche was on their reading list, and Kracauer invited friends to a Hegel reading group. Kierkegaard's existentialism was an important point of reference; it provided a philosophical undergirding for their reading of countless detective novels, and probed the manner in which these narratives enacted a "life bereft of reality."[4] They also devoured the writings of contemporary philosophers. Adorno sifted through the works of Georg Lukács, Ernst Bloch, Walter Benjamin, and Franz Rosenzweig. But, as with the real landscapes, Adorno cultivated a reserved attitude toward the intellectual land-scapes of his literary journeys. "I've read the *Elective Affin-ities* and found that I agreed with Friedel on its interpreta-tion, but less so with Benjamin, who has actually read into the text rather than reading something out of it, and blindly misses out on Goethe's substance,"[5] he wrote in reaction to Benjamin's essay on Goethe's novel. But that was only one example. In the early years, Adorno's intellectual energy of-ten flared primarily as a defense maneuver and a quest for self-assertion as the young whippersnapper of the group; of-ten he invoked the names of those he was striving to impress as derisive adjectives. Commenting on an acquaintance's presentation, he wrote to Kracauer: "what a murky Blochian confusion . . . how wrong, or at least how Benjaminian, how invariably metaphysics comes into play."[6]

These kinds of comments accord with the written ac-counts of Adorno's character from this period. Soma Mor-genstern's story of his long walk with Adorno to the streetcar Morgenstern needed to catch was probably exaggerated, but reveals something of Adorno's reputation; Morgenstern re-ports that Adorno talked incessantly, then stared in disbelief when Morgenstern had the nerve to climb aboard the street-car—after a proper goodbye—seeing as Adorno still had plenty more to say.[7] The composer Ernst Krenek, a more re-liable source, recalled Adorno as a "somewhat overly artic-ulate young man who seemed to be jockeying for my attention during the rehearsals for my opera *Der Sprung über den Schatten* [*The Leap over the Shadow*] in Frankfurt," but who "went on to become an edifying and challenging companion for many of the crucial years of my life."[8] The Adorno of the 1920s was a brilliant, precocious thinker whose genius got on other people's nerves; Adorno would later describe himself as endowed with "well-versed brashness." Adorno seemed fairly oblivious to reality, even to the reality of what others in his milieu were thinking.

Furthermore, the Naples trip seemed ill-fated from the start; indeed, it was a miracle that it happened at all. While Kracauer appeared established and successful on the surface, he was actually a complex, insecure individual. "I am an abyss, and as unsteady as a boy," he once wrote.[9] He was as yet unable to reconcile his metaphysical musicality with the excesses of the modernizing world; he practiced a "hesitant openness" in a state of expectation. Moreover, he had fallen head over heels in love with Adorno, whom he called the "lovely epitome of a human being."[10] He wrote to Löwenthal quite openly about this passion, "which I can explain to myself only in terms of my being homosexual in matters of the spirit."[11] In the early 1920s Kracauer had to stand by and watch Adorno, who—Kracauer insisted—was made up "in large part of Lukács and me,"[12] slowly but steadily outgrow his influence, become enamored with women, and, worse still, develop independent intellectual interests. Kracauer regarded these interests as true rivals. A previous trip to the Dolomites and to Lake Garda in 1924 had already been torture for Kracauer; his passion for Adorno was "truly noxious, and assumed frightening dimensions."[13] Kracauer tried to get over these feelings—and failed.

The crisis had escalated when Adorno went to Vienna

in March 1925 to study music composition with Alban Berg, a student of Arnold Schoenberg. Their correspondence during this period is a breathless document of the agonies and ecstasies of love and rejection; an innocuous tone could be (and was) interpreted as feigned optimism, and any kind word seemed to seal their split. Despite the precarious nature of their relationship, last-minute declarations and telegrams with plans ultimately made possible the trip to Italy in September 1925. Working on their relationship also dominated the trip itself, of course: "Being together with my friend is exciting and important in every way; it takes quite a toll on me personally,"[14] Adorno wrote to Alban Berg; and in 1928, when he traveled to Naples again with his future wife, Gretel Karplus, he sent Kracauer a letter from "our tragic haunts."[15] Even if Adorno had been more talented in apperceiving reality than he was, would there have been any time left to do so under these circumstances?

3

A Common Pursuit

In late September 1925—shortly before Kracauer and Adorno returned to Frankfurt after three weeks of travel through Capri, Positano, Ravello, Herculaneum, Pompeii, Amalfi, and Sorrento—a meeting with Sohn-Rethel and Benjamin took place in Naples.

Might this meeting have been no more significant than one of the usual "tiffs" about which Adorno later wrote: "We spent time together the way intellectuals used to meet forty years earlier, simply to converse and in doing so to tug just a bit at the theoretical bones they were gnawing"?[1] That depiction was somewhat euphemistic. More often than not, these theoretical bones also contained morsels of human discord.

The group consisted of two friends steeped in crisis (Adorno and Kracauer) and a virtuoso of the interior monologue (Sohn-Rethel), who recalled Benjamin's sharp means of expression during the meeting as the most terroristic act "I ever experienced mentally."[2]

Kracauer, who struggled with a stutter, would not have been able to keep up with this conversational pace. Benjamin was most likely still miffed by Kracauer's "editorial bullying" when his Baudelaire translations were assigned to Stefan Zweig for review for the *Frankfurter Zeitung*,[3] even though it was abundantly clear that Zweig was not up to the task. Benjamin wrote, "As far as S.K. is concerned: may God protect me from my friends; I can deal with my enemies on my own."[4]

And what could have been the basis of their conversation? The intellectual baggage that Sohn-Rethel, Benjamin, Kracauer, and Adorno were lugging when they met in Naples consisted of mountains of paper on the first two chapters of Marx's *Capital,* six hundred quotations from Baroque tragic dramas, detective novels as applied readings of Kierkegaard, and compositional problems drawn from the teachings of Arnold Schoenberg, which virtually none of them, apart from Adorno, could puzzle out. Could these ideas yield any sort of common denominator if each of the philosophical combatants was determined to keep gnawing monomaniacally at his own theoretical bone? What was the common language or the common diagnosis of the current era on which the four could agree? It was all fine and good to contend that bourgeois society was closing, but could they identify philosophical concepts that would enable them to analyze this closure, to ponder ways of establishing an open form of society?

Of the particular ideas discussed at the "philosophical battle," we have no record. But with the essays the members of the battle would write shortly thereafter, we can try to reconstruct the lines of reasoning and the points of dispute.

Sohn-Rethel could have helped us if he had only lifted his head out of the opening pages of *Capital.* Marx began his analysis with the commodity, the nucleus of the capitalist economic system. A thing becomes a commodity when it can be exchanged, if its use doesn't end as it is used but instead an exchange value is added. But in order to be exchangeable, the various commodities must be equivalent. According to Marx, the core of this equivalence is not a natural property of the commodity, but is determined by the labor performed to produce it. Commodities can be exchanged only if they can be traced back to a common measure—which is abstract, indiscriminate human labor. Another reader of *Capital*—though only his writing was present in Capri—used this concept of the abstract nature of human labor as a gateway to a sweeping history of decline. In Georg Lukács's view, as expressed in his book *History and Class Consciousness,* the process of establishing the equivalence of commodities was the disastrous key feature of the capitalist mode of production. He argued that any individuality, any quality that makes something stand out, is picked apart into small units in order to render it referable to something else. Streamlining the processes of production, which Marx could understand as emancipatory in contrast to the restrictive relations of production, resulted, in Lukács's view, in merely a "continuous trend toward greater rationalization, the progressive elimination of the qualitative, human and individual attributes of the worker."[5] The catchword "reification," used to describe this elimination, affects society as a whole: not only things that are produced, but also the judicial system, bureaucracy, the worker's soul, and so forth. For Lukács, the structure of commodity relations is "a model of all the objective forms of bourgeois society together with all the subjective forms corresponding to them."[6]

Lukács's variant of Marxist analysis is an apt expression of existential forlornness in a closing world. Kracauer, for example, regarded modern people as "shoved into an everyday life that turns them into henchmen of the technological excesses. Despite or perhaps precisely because of the humane foundations of Taylorism, they do not become masters of the machine but instead become machine-like."[7] After reading Ernst Bloch's review of *History and Class Consciousness* on the island of Capri, his views shaken to the core by his encounter with Lacis, Benjamin wrote to his friend Gershom Scholem "that several points of reference converged here: in addition to a personal one, there was that book by Lukács, which amazed me because Lukács proceeds from political considerations to an epistemology and arrives at principles that at least partially, and perhaps not quite as extensively as I'd first assumed, strike a familiar chord in me or validate my own views."[8]

An adaptation of the commodity form is also found in Benjamin's book on the origins of tragic drama, where he takes to an extreme the description of the arbitrariness caused by the exchange with unparalleled (and, for him, utterly atypical) clarity: "Any person, any object, any relationship can mean absolutely anything else."[9] Although Benjamin was referring to the use of language in Baroque allegories, the diagnosis of his own era was impossible to miss: "With this possibility a destructive, but just verdict is passed on the profane world: it is characterized as a world in which the detail is of no great importance."[10] This world is profane because it consists of nothing but depleted things that have been made profane. Hence, Benjamin's analysis of the contents of Baroque tragic dramas just addresses closed-off spaces—a world unto itself, devoid of any perspective that would extend beyond it. "The baroque knows no eschatology," he concluded.[11] And in his treatise on the detective novel, Kracauer stages the hotel lobby as a secular counterpart to the lost sanctity of a house of God. Transcendence has been dragged down into the domain of immanence; the higher entirely into the lower.[12]

When Benjamin, Sohn-Rethel, Kracauer, and Adorno met in Naples in 1925, *History and Class Consciousness* was just a year old. Another of Lukács's books, *The Theory of the Novel*, had been published a few years earlier and thus had more time to leave a lasting mark on these aesthetically-minded vacationers in Naples. In *The Theory of the Novel*, Lukács had yet to formulate his unease with the modern world in Marxist concepts, but he furnished an image to describe the meaninglessness of the post-epic world. The world made by humans has rotted away; it is a "charnel house of long-dead interiorities."[13] The things that surround us have become rigid and alien, like skeletons. The charnel house is a symbol of a world that has taken leave of its senses, for a modernity that has lost any attribution of meaning, any hope of transcendence. "Warmth is ebbing from things. The objects of daily use gently but insistently repel us,"[14] Benjamin once wrote. Did Benjamin, Sohn-Rethel, Ernst Bloch, and so many others stay at the Gulf of Naples and at the Amalfi Coast to soak in the last warm rays of an orientation toward life that had yet to become modernized and alien, to experience a porous landscape that somehow remained free of such rigidity?

Sohn-Rethel, who often explored the city with Benjamin, cast aside his theoretical asceticism in a series of brief essays, and reveled in his descriptions of Neapolitan resistance to modernization. The stereotypical donkey cart could bring traffic to a halt; technical equipment was constantly broken. Sohn-Rethel, who as a child had had ample exposure to the world of heavy industry through his mentor, Poensgen,[15] seemed to delight in a society that was not yet fully modernized—in the "agrarian underground of the city,"[16] a "very old ingrained world."[17] He bypassed any mechanized forms of transportation to climb Mount Vesuvius, conquering the volcano on horseback and on foot.

Was this the least common denominator that these philosophical ruffians could agree on when they gathered in Naples: grousing about the bleakness of the modern world, and savoring the feeling of finding themselves in a place where this bleakness had yet to descend so fully? Were they no better than the multitude of travelers who sought to unwind from the alienations imposed by modernity: to feel that they had yet to become skeletal and exchangeable?

4
Charnel Houses

In fact, the exact opposite was the case. Naples was not an alternative concept to cold modernity; it was its finest illustration—but one that provided a way forward and *through* modernity, not away from it. Lukács's metaphor of the charnel house, the ossuary of reification, was omnipresent in Naples. It would have been hard to find another place with more skulls of every possible sort—and those are only the skulls that made it to the surface. Under the earth lies the negative image of the Naples that is visible to us, because that is where stones are retrieved for use in construction. During the plague in the seventeenth century, these hollow spaces assumed a practical function as actual charnel houses, and a cult surrounding the skeletons and skulls stored there was established, one that has endured to the present day. The Neapolitans select a personal patron saint, adorning and watching over that saint's bones, hoping in turn to glean hints of what the future holds and gain reassurance that their wishes, large and small, will be fulfilled. We encounter an extreme metaphor for reification in Naples in an uncommonly friendly light: the charnel house becomes a guarantor for what seemed lost through reification: bonding, closeness, warmth, transcendence.

This mechanism applies equally well—this time unmeta-

Fontanelle cemetery, Naples. Dominik Matus, Wikimedia Commons.

phorically—to things that have been detached from their expected functions. The Neapolitans, ever the audacious masters of improvisation, turn nonfunctioning technical things
into a "treasure trove of broken objects" and join them together to form something new and surprising.[1] Sohn-Rethel
tells of a helmsman who uses the broken motor of his boat to
make coffee,[2] and of a dairy shop owner who turns inoperative motorbike parts into a device to "whip cream."[3]

Sohn-Rethel's descriptions echo the enthusiasm of Goethe, arguably the most famous German to have traveled in
Italy. "In these people I find the most vibrant and brilliant
industriousness, not in order to get rich, but to live free of
care,"[4] Goethe wrote about the Neapolitans in his *Italian
Journey*. Sohn-Rethel, the foster child of an industrialist,
lent a conceptual framework to this early statement about
the subversive industriousness of Neapolitans. The magic

of objects unfolds for the very reason that they are broken, or because they have been removed from their customary contexts. Lukács may have lamented the alienation that results from reification, but this very alienation sets the stage for something new and joyous to originate: "In much this way, the most complex technical instruments join together in this city to perform the simplest, yet unimagined tasks,"[5] Sohn-Rethel wrote. In this way, he argued, the estranged objects and the charnel house are imbued with the ability to lift themselves back up from their alienated and profane nature. Transcendence hasn't been lost; it has rather entered into the estranged objects. In his book *The Ideal of the Broken-Down: On Neapolitan Technique,* Sohn-Rethel recounts the manner in which something as profane as a lightbulb turns festive and "unites, in a saintly image, with the Madonna's aureole, much to the fascination of reverential souls."[6]

Naples was ideally suited as the place for Benjamin to finish the book on German Baroque drama, because its construction arises from this very mechanism by which the profane is converted to transcendence. The notion of interchangeability is only the first half of a dialectic of the technique of allegory as described by Benjamin. It immediately becomes clear that the diagnosis already contains the cure: all "the things . . . used to signify" acquire, by the very fact of their "pointing to something else, a power which makes them appear no longer commensurable with profane things, which raises them onto a higher plane and which can, indeed, sanctify them."[7] We learn that "the baroque knows no eschatology," but the sentence goes on to say, "and for that very reason [a] mechanism by which all earthly things are gathered in together and exalted before being consigned to their end."[8] At the end of his book on the German Baroque tragic drama, Benjamin stages the transformation of mountains of corpses and the empty mundanity of life into a graceful, divine act of salvation.[9] The Naples essay opens with an example of this mechanism: a disgraced, ostracized priest is able to use the first available opportunity to resume his religious duties.

The Lukácsian charnel house was a metaphor for a world full of dead things no longer useful to the subject. It features in Benjamin and Lacis's essay on Naples as a comprehensive structural principle. The central concept of this essay, porosity, is also a variant of the reification diagnosis, but now in a positive sense. "Porosity is the inexhaustible law of the life of this city, reappearing everywhere," Benjamin wrote.[10] Lacis and Benjamin traced this law down to every last detail; even the insipid iced juices exemplified porosity. Nothing can be itself, pure and simple; everything is interchangeable and signifies everything else—in the climate of southern Italy porosity comes across like this: "The stamp of the definitive is avoided. No situation appears intended forever, no figure asserts its 'thus and not otherwise.'"[11] The dialectic of the allegory enables porosity to create a scene of vitality, surprise, and detail. The fallen priest can bestow his blessings once again, holidays find their way into secular weekdays, private and public life are entangled. The result of nothing remaining itself is a massive "process of intermingling,"[12] in which shortcomings create a path to abundance. It is astonishing that in all the postmodern analyses of Benjamin there have been so few detailed conceptual studies of the term *porosity,* seeing as this term seems tailor-made to puncture romantic and ideological attributions of original totality or integrity without sacrificing descriptive power; in fact, the descriptive power is made possible by confounding the schemata of difference.

According to Ernst Bloch, who also visited Naples in 1924, watching a group of Neapolitans enter a restaurant and casually blend in with the conversations already underway was "a true lesson in porosity; there is nothing aggressive about it, rather all is friendly and open, a diffuse, collective gliding."[13] But porosity originates in something real and tangible. All it takes to experience this porosity is to skim your hands along the walls of the buildings in Naples, as Benjamin and Lacis did during their excursions there. It was tuff—Naples's special building material—that La Capria identified as the characteristic feature of the Gulf of Naples. During a volcanic eruption, magma shoots into the air. Steam and gases leak out while the stone cools, leaving cavities in the stone and rendering it porous. Some of this volcanic rock is called scoria and is often regarded as a waste product. The tuff, on the other hand, pieces of which collect to form larger blocks, is extraordinarily useful. Because it is porous, it is lighter than other construction materials and provides better insulation. Moreover, its relative softness makes it easy to shape into the desired form.

Porosity is a feature of the raw material, but it also defines the space. In hauling away the tuff, Neapolitans created the aforementioned catacombs, and on a grand scale, the city came to exhibit the same quality of porosity as the rock from which it was built. The German author Martin Mosebach, a flaneur in Naples decades later than Adorno and the others, wrote, "The caves in the Fontanelle cemetery were quarries. For centuries, the enormous mass of tuff was used here to carve out outsized ashlars, which required the Neapolitan Baroque architects to work with massive proportions."[14] He drew no distinction between the charnel house metaphor and the porous stone: "The bones of those once buried here, however, have long since decomposed into dust, into brownish crumbs that can no longer be distinguished from crumbly earth-colored tuff."[15] The building material is already skeletal, as are the rooms that result from its removal: "The columns or pillars spring up from the brownish earth like bones and disappear in the stone of the gently vaulted ceiling. New chambers open out every which way, like fossilized protuberances; the walls are like skeletons ridged with recesses and bulges."[16]

Lacis and Benjamin had led the way to this magnification of porosity, laying out the transformation from stone to spatial organization. No sooner had they discovered porosity than they saw it everywhere, even when they were nowhere near masonry. "Seen from a height not reached by the cries from below, from the Castell San Martino,"[17] Lacis and Benjamin noted the city's cragginess, and described grottos that served as living and gathering spaces. Almost imperceptibly, they shifted the focus from natural formation to cultural implementation in pointing out that Neapolitans *created* grottos by cutting hollow spaces into stone. Then Lacis and Benjamin's text sped along the route from nature to "sophisticated" architecture, from the composition of building materials to the resultant structures: "As porous as this stone is the architecture."[18] This brief sentence encapsulates the transformation of a landscape into a philosophy, the transition from nature to culture. Lacis and Benjamin then broadened the concept of porosity to encompass the lives of the people unfolding within these buildings: "Building and action interpenetrate in the courtyards, arcades, and stairways. In everything they preserve the scope to become a theater of new, unforeseen constellations."[19]

Once identified, the concept of porosity extended well beyond construction and architecture and became a descriptor for all the everyday phenomena that Benjamin and Lacis observed. Every depiction in the Naples text is infused with this principle.

In 1955, thirty years after the Naples meeting, when Adorno published a first selection of Benjamin's writings, he was accused of taking a biased approach, of suppressing the materialistic, Marxist Benjamin. In the 1970s Asja Lacis was "rediscovered" in this context, and the publication of her memoir, *Revolutionary by Profession,* was prompted in part by the need to put an end to discounting influences on Benjamin relating to communism.[20]

However we may assess Adorno's first edition of Benjamin's writings, his disregard for Asja Lacis's involvement in the essay on Naples is utterly incomprehensible. After all, his own theory benefited substantially from the auspicious intersection of two different theoretical approaches, deeply influenced by the level of nuance that Lacis had likely introduced into this intersection.

Benjamin certainly saw the idea of porosity through the lens of the theater, preoccupied as he was with Baroque tragedy, but those tragedies had been "proper" theater from a bygone era. He must have found it highly appealing to discover the theatrical element in the social structure of his immediate surroundings. As a theater practitioner, Lacis was an ideal collaborator, so it was no wonder that Benjamin and Lacis experienced Naples, one of the places where the commedia dell'arte originated,[21] as a "popular stage" with a variety of performance areas, theatrical scenery, and unexpected directorial ideas.[22] Lacis's training in theater had had a revolutionary angle, and she now wished to return the theater to the people—to convert it back from an elitist artistic event to a natural, socially relevant, and timely form of expression. Lacis was already experienced in conceiving the city as a stage; in Riga she had directed a historical revue that portrayed the struggle between rulers and the oppressed as "a grand parade of actors and other participants through the entire city."[23] Benjamin had also explored the potential of a similar sort of multivalent composition, a "structure of relations,"[24] even before 1924, in examining Hölderlin's poetry. According to Benjamin, Hölderlin's poetic technique made it possible to arrange dissimilar things in free association: "So that here, at the center of the poem, people, heavenly beings, and princes, plummeting, as it were, from their old orders, are linked to one another."[25]

So both thinkers were already primed to see the structural and philosophical possibilities afforded by the Neapolitan landscape. And with the Naples essay, Lacis and Benjamin turned its contents, the structure of porosity, into its form. Not only did they write *about* porosity; they did so in a porous way. Their essay did not set forth an orderly progression of causal argumentation; there was no back and forth between thesis and example, no ordered introduction, argument, and conclusion. Instead, the material was simply strung together, each piece of equal value and an equal share in the overall picture, without any broader framework.[26] In the end, there was no moral or summary to which the various descriptions led. The reader simply comes full circle, taking a careful look at the various stations of the panorama it presents along the way.

A comparison of Benjamin and Lacis's text with Ernst Bloch's "response" brings out the distinctive nature of this sort of structure. Ernst Bloch, who went to Capri in 1924 with the "slimy Germanic wave,"[27] and recommended Lukács's *History and Class Consciousness* to Benjamin, held a firm place in Kracauer's, Adorno's, and Benjamin's literary canon—in particular, his *Spirit of Utopia*. But he was also a dreaded usurper of theoretical ideas.[28] Still, he was so impressed by Lacis's and Benjamin's essay that Bloch referred to it by name in his article "Italy and Porosity"; not only did he incorporate Lacis's and Benjamin's central concept right into the title, but he also noted the existence of porosity using the virtually identical examples as Lacis and Benjamin—the blurring of contrastive pairs (sleeping/waking, children/adults, private sphere/public sphere), the absence of a discrete domestic sphere, the theatricality of the place.[29] The only new element he introduced was attention to the special flavor of Neapolitan speech.

But despite the identical subject matter, the texture of Bloch's essay is utterly dissimilar. Formally, Bloch filled the porous holes right back up, and in the process porosity becomes "all-encompassing,"[30] and, once again, "uniformly whole."[31] Bloch invokes the term porosity not as an augmentation of the "capitalist division of labor," but as a contrast to it;[32] he romanticizes porosity and makes it a conceptual trophy. This text is not an image composed of individual, disparate elements, but one that drives home a point.

Benjamin and Lacis also skirted the fact that the conventional German image of Naples is a distorted one, the perspective of tourists and visitors. Still, this aspect is only one of many divergences that combine to form their image of the city. Bloch addresses this error in his very first sentence ("people generally come to this country in the wrong way") and picks it apart in his essay.[33] No matter how visually impressive his presentation is, Bloch's depiction of everyday life in Naples—shaped as it is by porosity—is merely a collection of examples of the concept. Once he has introduced the concept right at the beginning, he proceeds to elucidate its cultural dimensions and its place in the history of art. For Benjamin and Lacis there is somewhere in the middle a minimal discussion of porosity, but overall, it is the self-evident and unobtrusive principle that weaves through each individual section. These sections remain on one, uniform level; their arguments don't serve to bolster, build on, or exemplify one another, no reflection from the realm of high culture intrudes on the picture of everyday life.[34] In the typed draft of the Naples essay, a blank line is the only structuring element. The paragraphs within the individual sections, which established an additional hierarchical level, were inserted later by editors at the *Frankfurter Zeitung*.[35]

The structural principle of Benjamin and Lacis's essay is derived directly from the material discovery of porosity.[36] Sohn-Rethel, who arguably suffered an even greater injustice than Lacis, since his share in the constellation was forgotten *altogether,* also achieved this stylistic transformation of unforeseen configurations in his brief essay "A Traffic Jam on Via Chiaia." The essay comes full circle in its associative concatenations, returning to the street in which a traffic bottleneck brings life to a brief, image-crafting halt. The hustle and bustle of Naples becomes the stylistic ideal of his own writing.[37] The messianic energy and the shift into transcendence find expression in the pathos of highly compact description.

A significant aspect of the great appeal of Benjamin's writings—their antisystematic nature, the openness of their compositional style, which allows for various interpretive possibilities—originated in the porous Neapolitan stone. It

was this understanding of Naples, and its attendant philosophical implications, that Benjamin brought to the philosophical battle. Darwin had used coral reef formations
as a structural model to keep his theory of evolution from
looking overly orderly and unnaturally hierarchical.[38] The
convoluted structure of the rhizome would later serve as a
combative metaphor for science that did not accept classifi-
cation systems.[39] Benjamin, Lacis, and Sohn-Rethel looked
to the holes in the porous Neapolitan tuff. And Adorno? He
turned this porosity into music.

5
Music from Volcanic Rock

It is unlikely that Kracauer, Adorno, Benjamin, and Sohn-Rethel gathered for the famed philosophical battle in a typical Neapolitan "political People's Café" described by Benjamin and Lacis, in which a prolonged stay would be "scarcely possible." They probably opted for a spot in "the confined, bourgeois, literary world,"[1] maybe even the lobby of the Grand Hotel Vesuvio, where Adorno and Kracauer were staying. But they may also have met at the popular Café Gambrinus, frequented by virtually all intellectuals vacationing there. This café was located right on Via Chiaia, where Sohn-Rethel observed the traffic jam.

All had read Lacis and Benjamin's text about the city of Naples, which the pair had written after their 1924 visit to the city, and which was published in August 1925 in Kracauer's *Frankfurter Zeitung,* just in time to serve as a handout for the battle of the minds. "The essay on Naples marks a decisive breakthrough for Benjamin, and back then it had an indescribable effect on a few people, including me," Adorno wrote,[2] but only in retrospect, in 1953. In 1925, he had been decidedly more reserved about the text. For a start, he asserted that Benjamin had written it alone. Before the group gathered, he wrote to Kracauer, "And who is Asja Lacis? The sister of Theodor Däubler or a kabbalistic *ibbur?*"[3]

He also considered the whole approach too extrinsic, too matter-based, too materialistic. Where were the categories of the personal dimension and the interiority of the individual? Even if one might wish to reject these categories as too bourgeois, they could surely still be put to good use in some way. The discoveries that an individual's aesthetic sensorium could make were too valuable to be thrown overboard in pursuit of an obscure "communal rhythm" in collective settings. So on one side of the philosophical battleground were the new guests with their categories of "the personality and inwardness of 'the individual,'" which Adorno had been driving at, in a Kierkegaardian manner, for years[4]— an overly articulate man, endowed with well-versed brashness (Adorno) and seconded by his stammering teacher (Kracauer); on the other, sparring partners who were better acquainted with Naples, who had already conducted formal experiments with the porous material of "long-dead interiorities": a master of intimidatingly cutting articulation (Benjamin), seconded by the monomaniacal reader of Marx (Sohn-Rethel). Benjamin's attitude was likely a tad sharper than normal; a few months prior, he had learned that his book on the tragic drama had failed to earn him the hoped-for postdoctoral degree. The force of its theoretical design and the intricacy of its execution went well beyond any academic strictures and was consequently turned down, yet this rejection served only to confirm Benjamin's feeling that he had produced something truly significant, notwithstanding the academic small-mindedness with which it was received. And because Rowohlt Verlag had agreed to publish the text, he needed to defend and refine its concept. Now they were back to gnawing at their theoretical bones, as one or the other of them had so often done in Frankfurt.

After the battle, Adorno was pleased. He would write to Berg that, in his view, he had emerged on top. On September 30, he left Naples feeling that he had finally acquitted himself well. The highlight of the year still lay ahead, with no apparent connection to all his impressions of southern Italy. In December, Alban Berg's *Wozzeck* would be celebrating its premiere in Berlin. The 1924 Frankfurt production of *Three Fragments from Wozzeck* had so deeply moved him that he applied to be Berg's music composition student. The trip to Naples did not end his close tie to Berg, his "master and teacher," as he addressed him in his letters, but it did mark the end of his time in Vienna. Now, after the stay in Naples, a thirty-six-hour train ride, and two weeks of rest and relaxation in Amorbach, he wrote to Berg with an idea: could Adorno write an article about the *Wozzeck* opera for the music journal *Anbruch*? Berg telegraphed his delight about this proposal, along with several wishes regarding its content and the blunt request that the text be accessible. Berg had now grown accustomed to, and comfortable with, what he referred to as *Wiesengrunds,* Adorno's typical paradoxical philosophical statements on potentially everything under the sun, especially on musical themes. But for the average music lover—"absolutely uneducated in matters of philosophy"[5]—it would be advisable for Adorno to express himself in terms that are "*readily understood.*"[6]

Adorno gave it his best effort, skillfully weaving all of Berg's textual references into the essay. Berg's wish for accessibility, however, was not a priority for Adorno. He had something special in mind for the essay on *Wozzeck*. Now that he had written a doctoral thesis on Husserl, which he regarded as nothing more than a required assignment, along with a good many music and opera reviews, he sought to make this essay the prototype of a new kind of prose that would mark a new beginning, or really *the* beginning, of his development as a writer.

On November 23, 1925, about two months after returning from Naples, he reported to Berg that he was finished: "May [the essay] give you a little of the joy it gave me: it is actually the first one I'm quite satisfied with, and certainly the first one that gives shape to my new stylistic ideal with some degree of purity."[7] He claimed to have written his essay on a Berg composition in the same way that Berg composed his music: "My most secret intention in the essay's use of language was to proceed just as you compose, for example, a quartet, which resulted in an extraordinary encounter between your manner of composition and my current intellectual stance."[8]

It truly was an extraordinary encounter. Regrettably, Adorno did not refer explicitly to *Wozzeck*'s style of composition, because it would have been a dizzying experience to find a perfect resemblance between interpretation and the object of said interpretation. Mightn't an essay on the opera *Wozzeck* constructed just like the opera itself be tantamount to hearing the opera?

This was the same relationship between object and analysis present in Lacis and Benjamin's essay on Naples, which attempted to give porous form to their portrayal of the porosity of the landscape. Adorno strove to achieve this very kind of correlation, and moreover, the object was structurally identical. Adorno described a quartet's composition as porous, although he stopped short of using the word. According to the essay on Naples, "The stamp of the definitive is avoided. No situation appears intended forever, no figure asserts its 'thus and not otherwise.'" In Adorno's characterization, the compositional style dissolves all identities, all states of being oneself: "The Quartet—at least in its second movement—no longer has any 'themes' in the old static sense. Permanent transition softens up every solidified shape, opening it to what precedes and follows, holding it in a ceaseless flow of variants."[9]

While Adorno had felt that he had triumphed in the philosophical battle, just two weeks after his trip, he had to concede that at the same time, a "strategic opening," a "regrouping of forces,"[10] had taken place. The initial result of this theoretical musing is the essay on *Wozzeck*. In this piece, the formation of musical porosities takes shape in a circular structure, as it had in the essay on Naples. Adorno was paraphrasing this structural ideal when he wrote that the *Wozzeck* essay was, "in contrast to earlier ones, not arranged according to 'surface connections' . . . but rather [found its balance] in the continuity of its intellectual thrust, of its—ideational—simultaneity and factual equivalence of intentions."[11]

Soon this newfound stylistic ideal of the simultaneity and equivalence of intentions would take center stage in Adorno's writings. In "Parataxis," his essay on Hölderlin written in the 1960s, Adorno would refer directly to Benjamin's concept of Hölderlinian assemblage when championing paratactic sentence structure as a means of fending off the "logical . . . hierarchy of a subordinating syntax."[12] In his programmatic essay that analyzes the essayistic form, he adopts this structure for his own style as well. A defining feature of the essay, he explains, is that "in a sense all objects are equally close to the center": "Its transitions disavow conclusive deductions and instead favor crosslinks of elements, something for which discursive logic has no place." Like Lacis and Benjamin's porosity, an "affinity with the image" accords with the essay, owing to its "constructed juxtaposition."[13] As Adorno worked on his *Aesthetic Theory,* this juxtaposition evolved into a manual for his own writing: "In essence, the book needs to be written concentrically, in equally weighted, paratactical parts arranged around a center that they reveal by means of their constellation."[14]

In light of this ambition, the *Wozzeck* essay is a disappointment. At first glance, its most unusual quality is its complexity. That Adorno introduces Alban Berg at the beginning of the text only in the context of his teacher-student relationship with Schoenberg may have derived from Adorno's strategic impulse to establish this critical approach as a group effort. In the second section, Adorno turns to a discussion of musical variation, arguing that the connection between Schoenberg and Berg is evident solely in their use of this musical technique. The third and final section broadens the perspective from the purely technical arena to the confrontational position Berg took in regard to musical tradition.

The essay as a whole may go into greater technical detail than comparable essays from this period, with metaphysical evocations of genius or musical atmosphere replaced by technical analysis, yet it lacks a new stylistic ideal. There is none of the descriptive intensity that we find in Benjamin and Lacis's essay. The first section serves as a conventional introduction, then the essay proceeds to use conventional rhetoric to survey and briefly size up the "contours and breadth" of Berg's "spiritual landscape in both of its directions." Had Adorno's newfound stylistic ideal failed to move beyond his initial enthusiastic conception?

6

Star Formations

Despite Benjamin and Sohn-Rethel's group's initial and excited embrace of the concept of porosity, the term itself is scarcely found outside writings specific to Italy. Benjamin used the term less and less often,[1] even though it would have been ideally suited to the phenomenon that would soon become the focus of his writing: Paris arcades as the porous layout of the shopping malls in the nineteenth-century metropolis.

Adorno's use of the term ebbed as well; he gravitated instead to the related but less site-specific concept of constellation, which had overtones far better suited to philosophical use. A term that encompasses almost infinite variations today, *constellation* technically denotes a celestial formation, but it can be drained almost entirely of this referent and become a rhetorical designation for a broad range of situations or relationships. As Adorno adopted this term, it came to offer him an exceedingly helpful semantic range.

In Benjamin and Lacis's Naples essay, the constellation designates both an architectural assemblage and a social culture. The connotation of star imagery also lends the "unforeseen constellations" a utopian touch. The star metaphor is not especially original; stars figured in a great many the-

oretical writings of the 1920s. In his monumental explora-
tion of Judaism, Franz Rosenzweig's *Star of Redemption* uses
the intersections and points of the Star of David to mark the
elements of his theological thinking. Lukács's *Theory of the
Novel* opens with a star-filled night: "Happy are those ages
when the starry sky is the map of all possible paths—ages
whose paths are illuminated by the light of the stars."[2] Benjamin, too, used the star image programmatically; his essay on Goethe's novel *Elective Affinities* ends with the now-
famous hope for the hopeless—the star "shooting" above
them as its symbol.[3]

But the constellation in Benjamin's body of work is more
than just another example of star imagery. It designates the
process by which something can take on the characteristics of stars while bearing no actual resemblance to them,
joining together broken, porous things to form something
"surprising and new," as Sohn-Rethel observed in his piece
on everyday culture. In their conceptualizations of the constellation, Benjamin and Sohn-Rethel added the factor of
collocation to this narrative, arguing that the transformation takes place, not on the level of the individual thing,
but rather in the combination of porous things—their *constellation*. The resulting star formation is more than a mere
index for something vaguely transcendent; rather, it represents a particular "truth" and hence a far more ambitious claim. The concept of the constellation served to ex-
pand the implications of the porous structure, no longer a
mere stylistic principle. In the "Epistemo-Critical Prologue"
to Benjamin's book on the tragic drama, which he was wrestling with when he met Lacis, the question of representation became the essential element of emphatic knowledge,

the truth of the object under investigation: "For ideas are not represented in themselves, but solely and exclusively in an arrangement of concrete elements in the concept."[4]

In an earlier version of the prologue, Benjamin tried out different metaphors as he zeroed in on this representational form of philosophical interpretation. At first he envisioned a mosaic, then the stones of Sinai, then motherhood, a vortex, and the sun.[5] But he did not land on the definitive image until the later version:[6] "Ideas are timeless constellations, and by virtue of the elements' being seen as points in such constellations, phenomena are subdivided and at the same time redeemed."[7]

On the level of content, the German tragic drama and Lacis's communist influences may have clashed, as the editors of Benjamin's collected works observed.[8] The swerve from a treatise on tragic drama to the *One-Way Street* is striking.[9] On the level of the objects under investigation there is, of course, an enormous difference between a discussion of Baroque nomenclature and the materiality of everyday life. Still, the hubbub of life in Naples finds its way into Benjamin's book on the tragic drama, even into its "Epistemo-Critical Prologue." He came to regard the constellation as the key to a new kind of interpretive technique, and he immediately applied it to the study at hand. The argument about Baroque tragic drama arises, not in an argumentative series of statements about specific elements, but in a simultaneity that brings together dissimilar elements. For Benjamin, the "idea" of the tragic drama does not aim at a definitive conclusion, but is instead presented in a constellational arrangement.[10]

The structure of a theoretical study designed in this way is consequently not fluid, but rather, as Adorno later com-

mented, "is so constructed that despite the extremely painstaking architecture of the whole each of the tightly woven
and internally unbroken sections catches its breath and begins anew instead of leading into the next one as required
by the schema of a continuous train of thought. This literary
principle of composition claims nothing less than to express
Benjamin's conception of truth itself."[11]

The open structure of porosity that made possible the
intensity of description in the Naples essay was now put to
good use as a constellation for a genuinely theoretical text.
Adorno also took part in this expansion of the constellation
to render it an instrument of philosophical interpretation.
In his inaugural academic lecture, delivered in 1931, Adorno
used the term *constellation* programmatically, yet there is a
notable semantic emptying out of the word: true philosophical interpretation, he insisted, has to "convey its elements
into changing constellations—or, to use a less astrological
and more scientifically current expression—into varying experimental arrangements, until they make their way into
the figure that can be read as an answer, even as the question disappears."[12]

The constellation has long since been identified as a central concept in interpretations of Adorno's philosophy, although it has been overshadowed by the other key concept,
the "dialectical image," and is generally regarded as the less
expressive synonym for this type of image (we will discuss
the dialectical image in later chapters).[13] While the vague-
ness of the term constellation makes it open to multiple
uses in the critical literature that followed, the concept remains oddly nebulous. So is the constellation, along with
those "varying experimental arrangements," really just carte
blanche for what Claude Lévi-Strauss has dubbed *la pensée*

sauvage (wild thought), unable to constitute any norms beyond a confrontation with ordinary rationality? Is it merely the lowest common denominator of the theoretical reaction to the pressure of an unwieldy modernity?

The participants in the Naples meeting in September 1925 were certainly not the first to formulate philosophical reactions to modernity. Later, Benjamin and Adorno would devotedly explore nineteenth-century pushes for modernization, which they most closely associated with the work of Charles Baudelaire. Their investigations exploited all possible metaphors for modernity, those that made allowance for a muddle, and those that acknowledged the complexity of a reality that could no longer be grasped in linear figures: the kaleidoscope, the prism, the web.

But for the thinkers who would go on to formulate Critical Theory, the primary metaphor for this complexity became the constellation—an image that would take on a life of its own for decades to come.[14] However, while the idea of the constellation appears to be a promising theoretical instrument, as a mere contrast to linear thinking it is far too broadly defined to yield precise rules of application. It seems to be the formal principle of aesthetic thinking, attainable through sensitivity and practice. Could it be that the truth of the *Wozzeck* essay is not immediately obvious to us for the simple reason that Adorno's talent for this art of representation was not yet fully developed at this time?

The following remarks will counter with a definite no. A clear regularity underlies Adorno's variant of the constellation. To track it down from the vantage point of Capri, we need to direct our attention a bit farther east, away from Naples and toward the Amalfi Coast. An unusual postcard will point the way.

7
Postcards

For all its excitement, tourism can be a tiresome enterprise. While Capri became the gathering place for nonconformists and drifters of all kinds, they did not remain a self-contained group for long. The very moment bourgeois society creates the dream of an unspoiled destination, Enzensberger contends, it undoes that dream. Even Kopisch had vigorously promoted the development of Capri as a tourist hot spot and, as "multimedia propagator of his discovery,"[1] envisioned recreating Mount Vesuvius or the grotto in the form of miniature models. Back in 1874, Theodor Fontane had remarked, with a touch of annoyance, that there was no escaping "the bluster of the thicket of German poets on this blessed patch of earth."[2]

Postcards played a major role in shaping the public imagination of these tourist hot spots. A postcard sent from an interesting location, with its typically modest informative value, is an appealing phenomenon of everyday culture, and as such it aroused Walter Benjamin's interest. In 1926, Benjamin was taken with Kracauer's brief essayistic portraits: "set pieces of petit bourgeois stagings of dreams and longings," such as the umbrella and the piano. If Kracauer continued to pursue these set pieces, Benjamin wrote to Kracauer enthusiastically in 1926, the two men "might converge at a point

I've been targeting vigorously for a year without being able to hit it right in the center: the postcard."[3]

But it would be Adorno who would actually execute this idea, albeit in an article that did not appear ideally suited for it—an essay on Franz Schubert, which he wrote for the journal *Die Musik* in 1928 to commemorate the hundredth anniversary of Schubert's death, shortly before another visit to Naples. The postcard, he writes, is part of a trend, dominant since the nineteenth century, of fashioning the "miniature landscape as an object for bourgeois use of every kind."[4] Adorno turned to the subject of the postcard in the framework of an essay on music because he compared it to the musical practice of potpourris, where musicals motifs are detached from their original context to create a new piece of music. For example, any selection of the "best of" a composer's work, which selects particular movements from pieces, but does not include the entire piece, is a potpourri. Potpourris are a singular musical phenomenon that help music achieve a second life, but the result is randomness. "The complete interchangeability of the individual themes there points to the simultaneity of all events that come together devoid of any history." According to Adorno, postcards, which came into existence at the same time as potpourris, are of this nature. They, too, are a "surrogate" of reality, displaying a world unscathed by the fractures of modernity and the scars of history.

His view is easy to agree with: postcards are intended to portray a world full of meaning. In the early days of postcards, people took pains not to let traces of decay or modernization detract from the idyll pictured on the cards. Vacation postcards were icons of the escapism that motivates tourism. When the critical theorists wrote postcards from the Gulf of Naples, they chose from a limited selection.

Adorno sent Kracauer his regards from "our tragic haunts" on the back of the same standard Naples postcard that Ernst Jünger had used back in April 1925 to tell his mother that "the weather has improved quite a bit" and "the cold wind is over with."[5] Benjamin purchased multiple copies of postcards with classic tourist motifs (such as Capri's *faraglioni* rock formations); these fell far short of the quirky novelties he sought out on later trips.

Due to the sparse selection of actual postcards, we have to look to Adorno's imaginary postcards to "see" which sort of card he would have chosen, given the chance. The Schubert essay furnishes us with exactly this sort of verbal postcard. Shortly before his 1928 trip, Adorno begins the essay with a fantasy by evoking an image of a crater landscape, with a mysterious figure emerging from the volcanic depths and reaching the daylight:

> Crossing the threshold between the years of Beethoven's death and Schubert's brings on a shiver of the kind that might be felt by someone emerging from a rumbling, heaped up, cooling crater into a painfully fine and filmy white light and becoming aware of dark, gossamer-spun plants appearing before lava shapes on bare exposed heights, and at last making out the eternal clouds on their path, near the mountain and yet far above his head. Stepping out of the abyss, he enters the landscape that surrounds it and makes visible its bottomless depths solely by defining its outlines with its vast stillness and readily receiving the light that the glowing mass had just swirled blindly toward it.[6]

This description differs sharply from the kinds of messages conveyed on typical postcards, adorned as they are with pristine landscapes and beautiful vistas. Adorno's imaginary postcard, by contrast, seeks the traces of history embedded in the landscape. A volcano is ideally suited for this purpose; when it erupts, there is no denying that something momentous and catastrophic has occurred. An eruption attests to the destruction of a landscape, and thus presents the ultimate counterimage to the bourgeois postcard. And is it a coincidence that a crater embodies the ideal form of the constellation? Adorno depicts Schubert's "circular wanderings" along this landscape in the course of the essay by invoking the essential characteristics of the constellation:[7] "The eccentric structure of this landscape, in which every point is equidistant from the center, reveals itself to the wanderer who circles round it without progressing: all development is its complete antithesis . . . and the dissociated points of the landscape are scanned in this act of circling without ever leaving it."[8]

If, as the title "Schubert" suggests, the essay seeks to uncover the truth about Schubert, and the constellation is the form that Adorno and Benjamin thought capable of circling in on the truth of the subject at hand (in this case, Schubert), the goal was complete right at the beginning of the essay. But the constellation landscape does not come about that easily; the cliché postcard image keeps intruding, and the path from these cards to the porous landscape appears to be quite an arduous one. The Schubert essay claims that the landscape of the postcard gets "shattered" once it is infernally reflected by the potpourris. That claim sounds utterly incomprehensible at first, but we sense where it is heading. There is apparently no way of avoiding the nuisance of the bourgeois postcard; indeed, it must be tackled head-on. According to Adorno, the destruction of the postcard-perfect landscape is the only means of getting to the true one; the shredded remainder presupposes something set to be shredded, so it is worth our while to take a closer look at the composition of these postcards, particularly because Adorno's essay comes at them with conceptual guns blazing: "In them, the idea of a timeless mythical reality is presented in demonically depraved form."[9] We are talking about a postcard here. Isn't this a bit of an exaggeration? How do myth and a demonic element find their way into this kind of card?

In order to see how this may be the case, we'll need to take a brief side trip from Naples to the town of Positano, south of Vesuvius.

8

Skeletons and Specters

Tourists escape in part to find seclusion, but because other tourists are sure to follow, they must constantly seek out new secluded places. During Savinio's stay in Capri, he climbed up Monte Solaro and shouted in delight: "pointed aloes and prickly pear border the path. But up here their broad, fat leaves are not disfigured by the dithyrambic outbursts of enthusiastic visitors. The wave of tourism has not spread this far."[1] Benjamin and Sohn-Rethel similarly found the tourist-resistant travel destination they were seeking in Naples. And in the 1920s there was yet another destination for those seeking to flee from the wave of tourism: Positano, on the Amalfi Coast.

Capri is the ideal starting point for every sort of adventure that includes the Gulf of Naples and Amalfi. Separated only by the Sorrentine Peninsula, both coasts are within easy reach. Depending on what travelers are seeking, they can pay a visit to the urban chaos of Naples or the pristine nature of Amalfi. All around Naples La Capria beheld the Virgilian landscape, marked by light tuff, while east of Sorrento, along the Amalfi Coast, he observed Homeric scenery, recognizable by the "geological and morphological otherness that suddenly crops up."[2] There, tuff gave way to limestone. La Capria wrote: "The stone abruptly becomes

Positano, on the Amalfi Coast. From Adolf von Hatzfeld, *Positano* (Freiburg: Pontos Verlag, 1925).

something compact, iron, and the dolomite cliffs plummet straight down into the sea, reverberating in the grottos. In this landscape one becomes aware of tellurian-like forces being unleashed."[3]

Those in search of a less polished atmosphere than in Ca-

pri—less permeated by monetarily charged aestheticism—
opted for the telluric landscape. Carved out of the moun-
tain, Positano emerged as the intellectual capital of the
Amalfi Coast in the 1920s. Before word got around that Positano was a more rugged alternative to Capri, the writer Alfred Kantorowicz characterized it as an "utterly remote and
unknown place."[4] Brecht's stage designer Caspar Neher, who
boasted of having discovered Positano, pronounced this
judgment: "It is a hamlet devoid of creature comforts, but
there is an abundance of scenery worthy of capturing in art.
There isn't the flashy beauty of Capri or Sorrento here, nor
are there the clichés associated with southern Italy. Nature
is rough here, unwieldy, bleak; it has the desolate appeal of a
landscape constructed with hardship and effort."[5]

Positano's somber atmosphere inspired many travel writers to focus their attention on its eeriness. Benjamin claimed,
with a touch of irony, that this mood resulted when "a mi-
grant intellectual proletariat meets up with a primitive in-
digenous community."[6] Kracauer, who also made a stopover
there with Adorno in 1925, remarked that "ghosts, bohemi-
ans, and dubious characters of every conceivable stripe"
haunted the place.[7]

Benjamin recalled the time that during a nighttime stroll
in Positano with Bloch and Sohn-Rethel, he decided to take a
short walk uphill on his own, into "one of the deserted parts
of town": "I felt myself slipping away from the people down
there, even though I remained close by, within earshot and
with a clear line of vision. I was surrounded by silence, by a
momentous desolation. With every step I took, I physically
forced my way into an event about which I had neither an
image nor a concept and that was loathe to tolerate me. Suddenly I stopped between some walls and empty windows, in
a spiny forest of sharp moon shadows. Nothing could make

me take another step. And here, before the eyes of my companions, who had melted away into utter incorporality, I experienced what it meant to come under a spell. I turned around."[8]

"If you should make a stop in Positano, do think of me,"[9] Kracauer wrote to Adorno in 1928 when the latter traveled there for the second time, but Adorno replied that he "quite deliberately bypassed" Positano.[10] The clandestine aspect of Adorno and Kracauer's personal history there added yet another dark element to his associations with the town.

Kracauer's essay on Positano, "Rocky Delusions in Positano," utilizes Benjamin and Lacis's idea of architectural porosity to portray the town as a spooky prehistoric landscape that bewitched visitors. Positano is nestled into the slope of Monte Sant'Angelo in the shape of a cone, with a cemetery somewhere in the middle that appears to "plummet straight down into the city. It is a hole into which coffins are tossed; simple boxes, their lids snapped shut over them."[11] During torrential downpours, skeletons could float from the vaults into gardens and houses; Kracauer described Positano as a "skeleton cell," a "necropolis whose skeletal houses slowly crumble in the stagnant air."[12]

More significant for the spooky atmosphere, however, is a different set of protagonists: ghosts and apparitions. For Kracauer, Positano was not only a city of the dead, but also a dwelling place for the *un*dead: "The gods may have departed, but the place is still haunted by old demons"; "revenants" roam about, "drifting through the ages, preserved supply," he wrote.[13] Kracauer may have chosen Positano for his travel essay rather than a place like Pompeii because the jarring environment was more alluring than the museumlike sepulchral silence.

Sohn-Rethel was quite familiar with the specters of the

town, having stayed at the home of an uncle in Positano in addition to the villa in Capri. And he kept encountering the specters described at the end of the first chapter of *Capital*. The section about the fetishism of the commodity stands out because it allows for ideological critique of even the smallest unit of the capitalistically organized economic system. According to Marx, the principle of the interchangeability of all produced commodities culminates in "magic and necromancy,"[14] a "fantastic form" in which the human labor expended on the commodities is reflected back as a natural property.[15] Things that are produced seem to be derived from nature: "products of the human brain appear as autonomous figures endowed with a life of their own, which enter into relations with each other and with the human race";[16] they assume a "fantastic form different from their reality."[17] For Sohn-Rethel, this stay in Positano also meant confronting one of the extreme excesses of Marx's imagery, which he probed with ferocious intensity for the benefit of scholarly accuracy: "I must keep on attaching importance to my once having spent a year and a half doing a precise analysis of every sentence of the first two chapters of Marx, extracting every term, scrutinizing its every characteristic, ascertaining when it should be taken literally or whether it was intended metaphorically. . . . What does the use of metaphors mean in this instance? How is it legitimized?"[18]

A few years before Sergei Eisenstein attempted to film Marx's *Capital,* and long before Jacques Derrida's reading of Marx, which placed Marx's specters in center stage, the critical theorists found in Positano the site of the specter-as-commodity. But while Positano emblematized the spectral space, revenants and demons were to be found in Naples as well, in the famous aquarium, which Anton Dohrn built and shaped into a site of international renown.

Anton Dohrn astride the fisherman Aniello Fontanarosa, 1890.
© Stazione Zooloogica Anton Dohrn—Archivio Storico.

In the 1860s and 1870s, Dohrn gained numerous advocates for his project, and the city of Naples gave him a plot of land in Villa Reale, a park directly by the sea. When it emerged that the running costs of the Zoological Station exceeded the revenue from the aquarium, he established a "bench system" by which governments could rent a workspace at the station and send researchers there. Freed from teaching and other obligations, scientists could develop a stimulating atmosphere marked by internationality and collegiality, with young scientists on an equal footing with established researchers at the "benches." This atmosphere remained intact even after World War I. Several months before Adorno's visit, Ernst Jünger, then a student, had traded cannons for microscopes.

Another element that proved essential to the success of the Zoological Station was the fact that Dohrn was not only a scientist but also an art lover. Like his father, he did not accept the notion of a division between the scientific and artistic spheres—and Felix Mendelssohn was Anton's godfather. One hall in the Zoological Station was to be reserved for the arts, for which Dohrn commissioned Hans von Marées to paint frescoes. This feature helped to make the aquarium a must-see attraction, at least for German visitors. Visitors to the Fresco Hall were asked to submit their calling cards,[19] which were stored in the research station. In the records for September 1925, there is Adorno's card,[20] a plain one bearing only this identifying information: "Dr. philos." Still, it was printed in modern minimalist sans serif. Kracauer, by contrast, turned in an impressive card in a bourgeois-style curlicued script, as befitted his status as an editor at the *Frankfurter Zeitung*; Sohn-Rethel, who had no card at all, had to enter his name—and his wife's—on Kracauer's card.

The four of them wandered through the Fresco Hall and paid a visit to the aquarium, marveling at "the ferns that bristle and wave, the choking polyps and the geometric patterns, the tubular systems that attest to an uncreaturely life. We are retransformed by them; they emerge from hell, they snap at the purer beings,"[21] Kracauer wrote in his essay on Positano. The shapelessness of these beings, we are told, is evidence of their impurity; often they appear as masses and are difficult to identify. The 1905 German-language guide to the Aquarium Neapolitanum called them "viridescent congealed clumps."[22] Back in 1902, the young Paul Klee, who was impressed by the aquarium, had observed many odd things, such as "a delicate little congealed creature swimming around on its back by twirling its sweet little tail in a back-and-forth motion."[23]

The strange inhabitants of the aquarium illustrate Marx's understanding of abstract human labor. In the opening pages of *Capital,* Marx discusses commodities, which have been abstracted from all use value: "Let us now look at the residue of the products of labor. There is nothing left of them in each case but the same phantom-like objectivity; they are merely congealed quantities of homogeneous human labor."[24]

In 1925, when Sohn-Rethel was writing his own essay in Positano, he found this abstract concept of abstract labor the main stumbling block in the imperfect theoretical formulation of Marx's ingenious doctrine; in his view, this was the last remnant of idealism. This "spiritual 'matter' of abstractly human labor" is the reason that Marx didn't manage to turn Hegel upside down;[25] it is the remnant of Hegel's absolute spirit, stuck at the "metaphysical locus of Marxist theory."[26] And Sohn-Rethel—with his characteristic zeal—centers on the question of what needs to take its place. "Alfred was the first to make me aware of the use of metaphor in *Capital,*" a later companion of Sohn-Rethel wrote, and the first of the terms he listed as examples was the "congealed quantity of human labor."[27]

One of the many astonishing things about Positano was that skeletons and specters—the dead and the undead—were on view side by side. This same juxtaposition was found, in

Salvatore Lo Bianco in his studio, 1889. © Stazione Zooloogica Anton Dohrn—Archivio Storico.

miniature, in the Naples aquarium. On display in the tanks were not only those hell dwellers, but also dead specimens of sea creatures. For the additional ticket price of one lira, according to Grieben's travel guide, which Kracauer carried with him, visitors could enter the "permanent exhibit of marine animal specimens."[28] Positano's "skeleton cell" had its disconcerting counterpart in this Neapolitan cabinet of curiosities.

This was no ordinary collection. It was a showcase, the presentation of an achievement that would become a key component of the Zoological Station's international renown. In 1874, Dohrn had brought in a young Neapolitan, the son of the doorman at the Villa Torlonia (where Dohrn resided) to work at the Station. The doorman had always worried about young "Torillo," as he was called; he always sat "hunched over books . . . or tinkered or [sketched] corals and other objects."[29] When Dohrn gave Torillo a job—there was always *something* to do in the Station—his father hoped that this employment would straighten out Torillo's quirky behavior. But Salvatore Lo Bianco (Torillo's real name) proved to have an unexpected aptitude for killing animals to make them suitable for preservation. That is not as easy as it sounds. The strangely shaped, lustrous organisms would shrink or lose their color if not killed in an expert manner,[30] which would make it difficult to pinpoint the nerve tissue that clearly contrasted with the flesh in the living specimens.[31] Lo Bianco was able to kill the animals in such a way that they retained their shape and color. At the age of twenty, he was made head preparator at the Station.

Lo Bianco's masterful skill in preparing the specimens also facilitated research on animals beyond the institute in Naples. His preparations became coveted exports. Heuss, Dohrn's biographer, wrote, "Lo Bianco's work brought world renown to the Zoological Station for producing the finest preservations."[32] It is no surprise that even in the 1920s the exhibition of these preservations continued to be one of the most sought-after attractions at the Station. Not only this— they proved crucial to Adorno's nascent philosophy.

9
The Art and Science of Insertion

Adorno took in many of the sights during his stay in Naples—but would his sightseeing amount to more than a tourist's amusement? Shortly before his departure, as we have noted, the group met, battled, and dispersed. After Naples, Adorno initially focused his thoughts on dead matter, captivated as he was by the structure of porosity and constellation. We have seen how, soon after his return home, Adorno attempted to make it the structural principle of the first text he truly composed on his own.

But he was unable to put aside his spectral thoughts. He could drive them away for brief periods, but they would soon return with a vengeance. In his mind, they were part and parcel of a momentous strategic reflection: while Naples's porosity was all well and good as a utopian concept, it lacked a counterpoint. The imaginary Naples of Lacis, Benjamin, Sohn-Rethel, and Bloch offered an alternative to bourgeois life. To the rhetorical question, "What is actually the precise opposite of porosity?" Bloch gave the pithy answer: "The bourgeoisie and its culture."[1]

In Adorno's imagination, an idea was slowly ripening: Couldn't spectral imagery be used to construct a marvelously precise model of the bourgeoisie? Before long, he had devised a distinction between a skeleton and a specter. The skeleton is a porous, dead object; a specter, suggesting life, is its opposite. The diagnosis of one's own era takes a subtle but decisive turn. The present is no longer simply a charnel house, but rather posits itself as an undead entity. Adorno used this notion to construct the concept of the mere semblance of life. In his speech "The Idea of Natural History," he would define the process that would give new meaning and alien intention to dead things bereft of meaning, for which he used the term *insertion:* "This second nature is a nature of semblance in that it presents itself as meaningful. . . . Second nature is illusory because we have lost reality yet we believe that we are able to meaningfully understand it in its eviscerated state, or because we insert subjective intention as signification into this foreign reality, as occurs in allegory."[2]

The obstacle standing in the way of the constellation is pinned down with theoretical precision: it is the bourgeois man who doesn't let dead things stay dead, but instead awakens the charnel house to a new yet merely illusory life, closing the porous holes back up and impeding the constellation of dead and broken things. Like Adorno's imagined postcard from Mount Vesuvius, this process of insertion is a souvenir from the Gulf of Naples, this time from Sorrento.

Sorrento is situated on the border between the Virgilian and the Homeric parts of the Gulf, between the porous tuff and the hard limestone. Travelers from Naples to Positano pass through Sorrento, and those heading from Capri get to the mainland most quickly by way of the Sorrentine Peninsula. Sorrento was the place where twenty-four-year-old Nietzsche, suffering from terrible migraines, broke free from the philological constraints of his professorship in Basel,[3] and recuperated under "a milder sky, among pleasant people, where you can think, speak, and create freely."[4] It was there that he began to write *Human, All Too Human,* his first book composed in an aphoristic style, and rectified the "total aberration" of his instincts.[5] In asserting that there were no intelligible worlds, he struck at the roots of any "metaphysical . . . need."[6]

But Sorrento was also the stronghold of the handicraft technology that Adorno used to formulate the opponent of porosity. A record of Adorno's 1930s' seminar on Benjamin's book on tragic drama contains this comment: "The word 'insertion' is no mere metaphor here; inserting intention corresponds to the technique of intarsia in the Baroque decorative arts."[7] Grieben's travel guide to Sorrento informs the reader, "Artistic wood carvings and intarsia are created here,"[8] and the Baedeker guide notes, "INLAID WOODWORK ('intarsia') in numerous shops, good and inexpensive."[9] For Adorno, intarsia was the opposite of porosity; in intarsia, an assortment of wooden pieces is inserted into a wood surface to form a motif. The motif (that is, the inserted meaning) lays claim to intrinsic value, but that value is still tied to the material. The image created in this manner is spectral, its alleged existence illusory. No matter how the motif stands out—at times appearing to be three-dimensional—it is confined within the framework into which it has been inserted.

But despite this discovery, Adorno was still missing a significant element in transforming handicraft into theory. In the end, it took a different craft to galvanize the connotations surrounding the nexus of life and death in a manner that would prove essential for his model: Lo Bianco's technique of preserving dead marine life.

"As occurs in allegory," Adorno wrote in describing the technique of insertion, indicating that this technique was

Inlaid woodwork from Sorrento.

also inspired by his reading of Benjamin's book on the tragic drama. The book was finally published in January 1928 after a lengthy delay, the year Adorno wrote the essay on Schubert and traveled again to Naples, this time with his girlfriend, Gretel Karplus.

Wouldn't anyone in mental or physical proximity to the aquarium exhibition think of the process of preparing the specimens when reading this passage about melancholy in the book on the tragic drama: that under the gaze of melancholy the object becomes allegorical because it "causes life to flow out of it and it remains behind dead, but eternally secure"?[10]

Anton Dohrn did not want Lo Bianco's knowledge to become too widely disseminated; only selected expeditions were privy to training by this master. At some point, however, it was no longer possible to withstand the sponsors' pressure, and Lo Bianco had to disclose his technique. The sober, professional tone of his brief publication makes for a ghoulish account of the process by which he killed the various individual species of marine fauna.[11] But even the specialists understood that the true secret was not a purely scientific one anyway. A report on Lo Bianco's innovations states: "In many cases, for example, it is of critical importance that the fixation solutions be added at the right moment, that is, when the animal is in a particular condition; because the onset of this process is dependent on many variable incidental circumstances and also varies markedly according to the specific individuals, the conservator's feeling, or might I say discretion needs to make the decision, and in this respect it is not so easy for someone to replicate what an experienced conservator does."[12] For Adorno, the refined manner in which these species were killed was already the aim of the critical endeavor. The "treatment" of sponges, for example, does not require any expertise; its desiccation is common knowledge. The aquarium guide explains the process: "To prepare sponges for this use, they should be left for several days to allow all their pulpiness to decompose."[13] The gelatinous composition dries up, until all that remains is the porous skeleton.

For the allegorist, this ebbing away of life is just the start. Once the object is dead, one can begin to invoke all kinds of meanings, as the object "is now quite incapable of emanating any meaning or significance of its own; such significance as it has, it acquires from the allegorist. He inserts it within, and reaches down there."[14] In the book on tragic drama, this is the only trace of Adorno's programmatic expression: "insert . . . signification . . . as occurs in allegory." This "insertion" accords well with the second half of the work of a conservator: things are not just left for dead, but instead shifted into an odd intermediate state between life and death.

Benjamin's brief report—written soon after the philosophical battle—about a 1926 James Ensor exhibition in Paris

James Ensor, *The Haunted Furniture* (*Le meuble hanté*), 1888.

demonstrates how the two crafts of "insertion," intarsia and preservation, reached a moment of alignment. Ensor's painting *The Haunted Furniture* (*Le meuble hanté,* 1888) depicts an interior and a reading child surrounded by eerie masks. The child appears to be merged into the background, which, in Benjamin's view, makes the painting resemble a "ghostly intarsia."[15] Benjamin employs the metaphor of masklike fish in describing this interior: "A dim light breaks through heavily draped windows into the interior of those chaotic rooms overcrowded with furniture in which we, as children, were often close to suffocating, as though in the entrails of a reptile." These were still lifes "on which fish, for example, already turn masklike."[16]

James Ensor, *The Ray* (*La raie*), 1892.

This metaphor was not chosen at random; the set of mo-tifs drew on Ensor's childhood home in Ostend, which dis-played a group of maritime collectibles that included "star-fish, preserved deep-sea fish."[17] According to Benjamin, the masks that create the effect of an eerie assemblage in the intarsia image are prefigured in Ensor's oeuvre by fish that have become masklike until they were ultimately emanci-pated from their origin.

We have come quite a bit closer to understanding why Adorno characterized postcards as mythical in his essay on Schubert. The postcard is initially smuggled into the essay as a Biedermeier-style genre postcard, rather like an ideo-logical accompaniment to highlight the kitschy side of Schu-bert.[18] And so the postcard also reflects what is subject to criticism regarding the potpourris, namely that they present all possible musical motifs at once, and history does not appear developmentally in them. They hold out the promise of a "second life" yet are mere "surrogates." The new life is only an artificial construct, which makes the bourgeois postcard an astonishing thing. We see a world that is only apparently alive, an appearance that Adorno called mythical for the first time. But how does this second life take shape "in demonically depraved form"?

Adorno's model of the insertion of artificial meaning into a dead and alien thing is not a static process; instead, the thing affects the meaning with its deathly chill. For this process, too, Adorno draws on Benjamin's book on the tragic drama, which bears metaphorical traces of their experience in Naples. In Benjamin's book, we read that writing, the carrier of meaning, has "nothing subordinate . . . it is not cast away in reading, like scoria. It is absorbed along with what is read, as its 'pattern.'"[19] And the inserted meaning can no longer shed this "pattern." This is the materialist revenge on the idealistic insertion of meaning. Anything metaphysical that seeks to draw attention to itself in the world needs something visible to root it, just as the image of inlaid woodwork cannot be separated from the material. The spirit (in the nonspectral sense) "remains bound to the body as its expression,"[20] Adorno would later write in his book about Søren Kierkegaard. In the case of charnel houses, however, these physical shapes are all dead, and they transform the spirit that must make use of them into a demonic specter.

In Adorno's texts, this migration of death into the inserted meaning produced what came to be referred to as the "dialectical image." Subjectivity takes possession of dead things "by inserting intentions of desire and anxiety into them. Insofar as these departed things stand in as images of subjective intentions, they present themselves as stemming from the primal past and eternal. . . . While the things are roused in appearance to the very newest, death transforms meanings into the oldest,"[21] Adorno later wrote to Benjamin to clarify the concept he believed to have learned from him.

When Adorno and Kracauer gazed at the strange corpses in the collection of prepared specimens and the tanks with living animals, their narrative fantasy turned the latter into demonic spawn of the inserted specimens. The insertion of meaning produces an appearance of life, but the deathly quality works its way through the artificial life and makes it a demonic reflection, which is why Kracauer regarded these sea creatures as "emerging from hell." In this same vein, Adorno's Schubert essay could call an innocent postcard "demonically depraved."

For Adorno, the altered diagnosis of the state of the modern world and the mechanism of the dialectical image transform the setting of the theoretical imagination. We are no longer subjected to a charnel house, surrounded by dead and alien things. We are among the ghosts, floating through a spirit world full of the undead. This variant of hell is possible because dead things have been given an illusory life, the setting populated with demonic creatures that straddle the boundary between life and death. There is not a pile of corpses, but instead a maximal negation of anything corpselike: "the inability to die as negative eternity."[22] Fortified by his reading of Benjamin's book on tragic drama and the products of Kracauer's meticulously detailed imagination, Adorno turned his experiences of eerie Positano, Sorrentine

Tourist advertisement for the Aquarium Neapolitanum, 1902.
© Stazione Zooloogica Anton Dohrn—Archivio Storico.

handicrafts, and experiments at a marine biology research station into philosophical thought.

This hellish scenario found expression in powerful and enticingly suggestive imagery in Adorno's writings, but it impeded his path to the actual goal he was after, the constellation. A bourgeois longing for meaningfulness results in plugging up the holes of porosity, and the party responsible for impeding the constellation becomes visible. But if the dialectical image impedes the constellation, is there any way of getting to it?

We may well be closing in on what we're seeking. Two dialectical images are employed in the Schubert essay: landscape postcards and potpourris. The latter assume the astonishing function of shattering the "ambiguous eternity" of Schubert's landscape "so that it can be recognized. It is the aforementioned landscape of death."

So our assumption was correct. The landscape that opens the essay is also where it is headed: to the constellation of truth about Schubert. And the potpourris are the driving force behind its creation, because they destroy the postcard landscape and turn it into a crater landscape by furnishing an "infernal reflection" of the postcard landscape. But how does that work, and what exactly does it mean?

The process of unmasking bourgeois man as a demon could serve a useful purpose for traditional Marxists, who might welcome this identification of the class enemy, then leave it to the proletariat to tackle the critical task of battling this bourgeois man. Still, Adorno had no interest in that angle in the early stages of formulating his theories. Instead, he framed bourgeois man as both the recipient and implementer of the criticism, impossible as that might be; how, after all, might someone caught in the sphere of illusions manage to break out of it, then criticize the basic conditions of his own existence on the basis of this very sphere? When Adorno later expanded bourgeois rationality to encompass all of humanity, Jürgen Habermas accused him of "performative contradiction." This accusation might appear plausible on the face of it: how is it logically possible to harness reason as a means of criticizing reason? In Habermas's view, a critique of ideology applied to itself describes "the self-destruction of the critical capacity [as] paradoxical, because in the moment of description it still has to make use of the critique that has been declared dead. It denounces the Enlightenment's becoming totalitarian with its own tools."[23]

Adorno's concept of the dialectical image offers an ingenious resolution to this contradiction. The image creates a target beyond one's own entanglement, possible to see this only in the reflection of one's own demon in something else.

For one brief moment, the wall of obscurity is ruptured and the truth about one's own condition is recognized. "You are disgusted by yourself," Kracauer wrote. "But that is what it is all about: that an encounter takes place here between creatures that do not actually exist, that you, who are also a phantom in the vacant void, are also haunted by bewitched figures who bar you from passing through and pull you into their forlornness."[24]

Once the subject has encountered itself in a dialectical image, it could undo the process by which meaning had been inserted.

In this instance, improvement by means of self-awareness could only signal that the cause of evil has been eliminated, which is to say: oneself. It is all fine and good to regard oneself as natural, but only at the time of one's own death does the subject take back the intention it has inserted and release the matter—and only then does the gelatinous creature dry out and become a porous sponge. "You could well imagine— and it isn't hard to picture—a young fellow committing suicide at the sight of the phantom," Kracauer wrote.[25]

Perhaps Adorno's most poignant thinking on this subject is found, again, in his writing on music. In his middle years, Beethoven had been the archetype of effervescent subjectivity, but as a dying man he became a model of how to counteract his own tyranny. In an essay on Beethoven, Adorno writes, "The force of subjectivity in late works is the irascible gesture with which it leaves them. It bursts them asunder, not in order to express itself but, expressionlessly, to cast off the illusion of art. Of the works it leaves only fragments behind, communicating itself, as if in ciphers, only through the spaces it has violently vacated. Touched by death, the masterly hand sets free the matter it previously formed . . . hence the conventions no longer imbued and mastered by subjectivity, but left standing."[26]

The dead things are freed up once the subject has retreated, and are eventually so fully undisturbed in their state of death that they can be pieced together to form a constellation.

10
Blasting Out Living Space

The man behind the blasting of hollow spaces in the south of Italy—a Swissman named Gilbert Clavel—was arguably the most alluring character Adorno and Kracauer encountered on their trip. Clavel suffered from curvature of the spine and tuberculosis; like many others, he had traveled to the south of Italy with the aim of improving his health. Two years after Adorno and Kracauer's visit, he died at the age of forty-four. The futurist painter Fortunato Depero, who enjoyed a close artistic friendship with Clavel, portrayed him in these terms: "a short hunchbacked gentleman, with a nose as straight as a little monkfish, with gold teeth and feminine shoes; his laughter was vitreous and reedy."[1]

Clavel was a universal artist. He wrote several stories and a short novel, *An Institute for Suicides,* which was published only in an Italian translation and reads like Kafka on drugs. The institute in the title offered three different means of committing suicide in a state of hallucination: binge drinking, overindulgence in sex, and opium. Together with Depero, who illustrated this "suicide institute" book, he developed a so-called plastic theater, the prototype of which, *Balli plastici,* was performed to great acclaim in Rome, then never again. But Clavel's greatest work of art, which he worked on for the last twenty years of his life, was an old "Saracen" tower in Positano.

There was no lack of oddball construction projects in the triangle of Naples, Capri, and Positano.[2] Anton Dohrn's aquarium had been an earlier monomaniacal project, and the most famous by far was Axel Munthe's Villa San Michele, a garden estate with spectacular views of Mount Vesuvius, the city of Capri, and the entire peninsula, its interior decorated with ancient art. Tourists to Capri with enough time could also fit in a visit to the remains of Tiberius's Villa Jovis or the nearby Villa Lysis, which had belonged to the flamboyant Baron Jacques d'Adelswärd-Fersen, who committed suicide in 1923 by overdosing on drugs. Stefanie Sonnentag provided a brief description of the man and his grandiose villa in her guide to Capri and Naples: "He devoted himself, in love and pain, to this ostentatious building with its Doric vestibule, the inwrought gold-plated mosaic of four fluted columns gleaming in the sun."[3]

Positano also differed from the villas in Capri in the peculiarity of its living arrangements. Although it, too, had "proper" homes, such as the one belonging to Alfred Sohn-Rethel's uncle Karl, there were also abodes of a more elemental nature. Alfred Kantorowicz, for example, wrote that he was living "in a remote vault carved into the cliff of Monte Angelo, vacant for centuries, unfurnished apart from a cot, a wobbly table, and two rickety chairs I had borrowed, a hundred meters above the sea."[4] In Positano, the hollows that Benjamin and Lacis had discovered in the rocks of Naples as they set out from San Martino were inhabited by guests from the north seeking an escape from civilization.

Gilbert Clavel combined luxury with primitivism as he cut into the rock of the tower to create a spectacular palace.

Everything about the project was remarkable. The Amalfi Coast has several of these towers. Gilbert's brother René later claimed that among all the towers they visited, none had such an odd pentangular shape.[5] At the time it was purchased, the tower was isolated on a cliff on the coast, so the only way to reach it for the early stages of the work was by sea. "When it was in a state of decay," the tower had become, as Kracauer wrote, "a cracked tooth; Clavel drilled it down to the root and placed a crown on it."[6]

The building venture became Clavel's artistic project of a lifetime. "For my brother, the entire construction of this tower was an architectural problem in which he effectively crystallized his intellectual ideas," René Clavel wrote.[7] There were more people at work on this tower than Kracauer suggested in his essay, but even so, the whole enterprise was headed by a self-educated man who "developed his architecture on his own and acquired his practical knowledge in close to twenty years of construction work with his foreman," as René pointed out.[8] To form a thirty-five-meter-long spiral path into the sea, for example, Clavel worked without the aid of any sketches, using only a compass and a divining rod.

Kracauer and Adorno had chosen an opportune time to visit Clavel in 1925; the tower was already habitable and open to visitors. The incomparably beautiful setting, coupled with the modern practicality of the interiors, was bound to impress. The *Berliner Illustrirte* had already reported that the tower and premises constituted "one of the most magical estates and one of the most magnificent examples of rock-cut architecture in the world."[9]

Even so, the construction work was still in full swing in 1925. Adorno and Kracauer were witness to the spectacle of

The Positano tower in 1909.

The tower after its expansion by Clavel.

Clavel attempting to construct several apartments around the tower, rooms in the rocks behind it, and secret passageways connecting everything. His method of choice—blasting—made the whole thing a marvel to behold. Under the circumstances, blasting was the only possible technique, and in the area of Naples it was a standard stage in building construction: "First the rocky ground was blasted in order to install an underground cistern, which was indispensable for collecting rainwater. The shell was constructed using the stones that resulted from the blasting and the mortar made up of pozzolan and limestone," as Claretta Cerio described the procedure.[10] This was the same method the Neapolitans had used to obtain building materials from the earth, though it was now carried out somewhat more rigidly.

The method was developed in response to what La Capria referred to as the "geological and morphological distinctiveness" of the material. Limestone is a sedimentary rock, and the lime minerals are organic sediments, or residues of chemical processes. Limestone is less porous than tuff. As John Grotzinger and Thomas Jordan write in their 2014 book *Understanding Earth,* "Buried sediments are . . . continuously bathed in groundwater full of dissolved minerals. These minerals can precipitate in the pores between the sediment particles and bind them together—a chemical change called cementation. Cementation decreases porosity, the percentage of a rock's volume consisting of open pores between particles."[11]

Accordingly, Clavel used blasting as a natural approach to construction, and the collateral damage caused by stones flying out too far was totally normal. His brother brought him a tip from America on how to minimize this problem: "In New York they placed big mats made of braided cables onto the explosives, and the mats flew up, but they prevented the stones from flying around among groups of buildings."[12] So this blasting technique was not unique, nor was it the sole construction technique. Cement supplies, sealing agents, and wooden bows were also employed, but blasting was the most challenging part: "The hollows are quite time-consuming to create and, as always, take more effort than the construction."[13] We can easily imagine that for visitors who stopped by, blasting was the most spectacular aspect of this expressive architectural feat.

Kracauer's description of Clavel indicates what a strong impression this visit made. Later we will see how Kracauer portrays Clavel as a demon of the very sort he was battling. But for a brief moment, Kracauer's poetic essay on Positano turned this short hunchbacked builder into a freedom fighter, and all the blasting into this fighter's most formidable weapon.

In Kracauer's imagination, the enemy that Clavel tackled was water, the very element that blocked the pores of the stone; the monstrous, gelatinous creatures inhabiting these waters were on view in the aquarium. Quite possibly Clavel's remarks to Kracauer and Adorno about the seawater at the time of their visit resembled this entry in his diary: "I see water columns spray out into dust before the rocks. Mountains of foam rush over sharp heaps of stone, and they swoosh right back disjointedly. This destruction occurs thousands of times a day, and thousands of times a day a new force changes flakes of foam into crests of waves. What are days, what are people and their years? In a quiet summer night a rock is submerged, quite softly, quite softly."[14] Clavel, alone in his tower, braved one destructive storm after another, with the sea at times resembling "a gaping pus-filled wound of a bloody brown writhing animal's body."[15]

Kracauer's text refers to the "seawater, a nymphlike mystery,"[16] whose influx is "drenching and destructive," which can be coped with only by blasting hollow spaces. The "open pits" achieved by blasting, Kracauer writes, are the single means of preventing this destruction, and "artificial hollow spaces are the only way to curb its salty attacks."[17] The gelatinous blob in the water is blasted away to the charnel house, the stone is once again porous, and the permeability that the critical theorists used to craft a social and epistemological utopia is restored.

"It is nighttime, and the fishing boats shimmering out in the distance through the dark expanse are bright lights. One, two, three, more and more—form into figures, constellations. The sky above them is just the same; bright stars above and below? I forget that the sea is beneath me; I see only the lights," Gilbert Clavel wrote in his diary.[18] With the lifelong architectural project of a Swissman inspired by Futurism and his deftly poetic description in Kracauer's essay, the standard Neapolitan construction method of "blasting" became a central metaphor for Adorno. All that has become second nature in the process of insertion and all that has become demonic with the appearance of the scoriaceous figure has been burst asunder.

11

Touring the Crater

Back in Germany, the premiere of *Wozzeck* in December 1925 was a resounding success for Berg. Adorno attended the premiere and accompanied Benjamin to the second performance, after which Adorno sent a letter to Berg with a detailed report.[1] A performance opens up new insights that cannot be gleaned by merely studying the score, and the insights that Adorno gained from these performances were so extensive that he weighed the possibility of writing an additional essay on the opera. But there was one more reason for him to try to articulate the truth of Berg's opera again: the philosophical battle in Naples remained at the forefront of his mind. The "mental regrouping" was in full swing, and had even increased in intensity: "Since autumn of last year—and the major dispute with Walter Benjamin in Naples—my philosophy has been in the throes of an intense development, the first signs of which were already evident in the [*Wozzeck*] essay published in *Anbruch*. After I devoted great energy to thinking it over, however, the incompleteness, the inadequacy of my previous categories hit me more and more powerfully," Adorno wrote in March 1926.[2]

In his earlier *Wozzeck* essay, the solitary subject—which he referred to as the expressionist subject—seeks to give expression to his suffering and isolation, but is situated in a musical tradition that has already used every possibility and hence rendered it unusable for any subjective, original expression. As Adorno saw it, the artist, in his drive for musical expression, needs to keep splitting apart the material until a transformation takes place. The musical material is emancipated as it is split apart by the composer's expressive desire that produced the fragmentation in the first place. And if the composer wishes to share in this process, which he reluctantly initiated, he needs to replace his expressive suffering by a "constructive will": "At the moment in which punctual harmony and its constructive form correlate under constructive will emancipates itself from the rule of psychological expression, a change occurs." With this change, however, the composer becomes a Clavel, who blasts away himself as well: "The blasting individual ceases to be a mere individual."[3] This is, once again, the compositional achievement that Adorno deemed fully realized in Beethoven's late style. It is not an emancipation on the part of the subject—who actually retreats—but rather an emancipation by the musical material itself, which is rendered porous in this change.

But it was this very change, this catastrophic collapse of the subjective intentions, that led to the creation of the porous constellation, the "theological reality content,"[4] the truth Adorno encircles as the center of the *Wozzeck* essay. It now becomes apparent what Adorno's earlier essay on *Wozzeck*—below the surface, which reads like a conventional piece of writing—actually "constellates." It presents an array of variations on the change, the subjective collapse, the catastrophic blasting, the creation of porosity. Just as in Benjamin and Lacis's essay on Naples, we encounter porosity as a stage, a hole in the center that is circumscribed as truth. But this truth is only the truth about becoming porous—collapsing—and this "truth" is encircled by a constellation made up entirely of small porosities.

The individual sections of the essay are all variations on this constructive center, which is to say, variations on the collapse. In the first paragraph, the change takes us from a traditional teacher-student connection to the isolation of both teacher and student, in light of which only musical craft can be passed on. This craft is the technique of variation, which is discussed in the second paragraph. In traditional music there is an essential distinction between theme and variation, but in Schoenberg's technique of variation, the variations stand out so prominently that in the end, there are no remaining independent themes. This is porosity in the purist sense, its very definition, as supplied by Benjamin and Lacis in their essay on Naples: "The stamp of the definitive is avoided. No situation appears intended forever, no figure asserts a 'thus and not otherwise.'"[5] In the third section the duel between the artist wedded to originality and the tradition that resists leads to a constellation of the wreckage of the musical forms. At the close of the essay, Berg's prior compositional oeuvre is even presented as a transition, a continually fruitful collapse, and the *Wozzeck* opera as a transition to the chamber concert, that is, as the material that becomes relevant for the constellation of the chamber concert.

The newfound model for philosophical interpretation and essayistic stylistics was thus almost fully developed in the early essay on *Wozzeck,* although it lacked one essential link. The second nature of the musical convention that the composer seeking expression rises up against and blasts through in the process of withdrawing from it had yet to be linked to the mechanism of insertion, of turning demonic.

While writing the first essay in the autumn of 1925, Adorno had discovered and attempted to implement a new stylistic ideal, but with his second essay on *Wozzeck* he realized the overambitiousness of his objective, and soon found himself confessing to Berg that he would not be able to make good on his plan to write it. Adorno sketched the path he had undertaken—including his approach to communism—"from the metaphysical starting points through epistemology through to a positive philosophy of history and political theory."[6] Adorno floundered at first as he tried to sort things out. Because he was still setting his sights on becoming a composer, he began by focusing on constellations, which he had transformed into a technique for both writing and composing, as he realized "that in music nothing is more paramount than the formal constructive imagination—more paramount indeed than the personality and interiority of the 'individual element' itself (which it of course presupposes dialectically!) that I have been harping on for years in a Kierkegaardian manner."[7]

But as time went on, Adorno augmented this model with a demonic element. In the first essay on *Wozzeck,* the infernal reflection had yet to surface.[8] In his second essay on this opera, which he managed to complete against all odds in 1929, the abyss from which the demons rise up as objective characters is "subjectivity."[9]

The essay on Schubert, written one year earlier, had already included as its central image the encounter with one's own demon, emerging from the crater of the volcano, although this scene is enacted, not by a subject, but by the object under investigation itself. Still, the—alleged—process is the same: The potpourris, the dialectical image reflect the demonic element of an ambiguously eternal postcard landscape and compel it to elicit its truth, to form a constellation of its own. In accordance with the hellish setting, it does so "infernally," forming a landscape of death. To understand this fully, we must also wend our way up Vesuvius.

Ascending Mount Vesuvius would seem to offer us relief from the age-old tourists' dilemma: if something as powerful as a volcano can't furnish the unique feeling that undertaking this journey was meant to inspire, then what can? Kant's *Critique of Judgment* had already grouped "volcanoes, with all their destructive force"[10]—along with bold cliffs, hurricanes, a raging ocean, and other dangers of this sort as a catalog of natural phenomena that could arouse the feeling of the sublime in us, but only if "we are in a safe place."[11] Those who were afraid, Kant tells us, "cannot pass any judgment on the sublime in nature,"[12] as they would be preoccupied with the more mundane matter of clinging to life. At long last, then, the tourist can enjoy a genuine advantage over the locals: while the latter live in the danger zone of an impending eruption, a guest—who spends the rest of the year in safety—can revel in a sublime shudder. "Hence for Kant," Boris Groys has written, "the subject of infinite ideas of reason is, first and foremost, the tourist."[13]

But in Kant's day, Vesuvius was not yet in the clutches of Cook's funicular railway. In 1887, John Mason Cook—the son in Thomas Cook & Son—purchased the railway that had opened eight years earlier. Shortly before Cook died, he launched the project of linking an electric railway to the funicular. Although Vesuvius staged a revolt in 1906 as it erupted, destroying the last section of the track, making travel on horseback necessary for the final portion of the ascent, this partial section was rebuilt three years later. The vehicle fleet was also increased by two cars, and newly installed electricity made night travel possible. In the 1920s the throng of visitors grew so large that three more cars were added.[14] The concept of package tourism made it possible for everyone who booked a trip to central or southern Italy to get a coupon for the ride up Mount Vesuvius—whether they wanted one or not.[15]

The trivialization of the sublime nature of the volcano went hand in hand with these technological advances. Even Theodor Fontane crossed off a visit to Vesuvius from his travel plans,[16] opting instead to use the volcano as a metaphor for his digestive problems. Gilbert Clavel came to envision Vesuvius as the motor of the vehicle that was his body: "I have just stuck a longish tube into the exhaust pipe of my deposit-laden bowel and poured in some light healing tea. A Vesuvian eruption ensued, which then turned my behind into a riflescope."[17]

This may be why Adorno opted for an unconventional path in climbing Vesuvius: The visitor at the start of the Schubert essay comes from the other direction, namely *out of* the abyss. When the Schubert essay turns to the subject of the crater's abyss and the chthonic depths from which the visitor emerges, it appears to be a deeply unhappy place. Once out of the abyss, the visitor can receive the light that "the glowing mass had just swirled blindly toward [the landscape]." In the abyss there is a force with an enormous level of activity, yet incapable of offering a view to the starlight. The stars shine only for those who have escaped the abyss, while the "zealous hand" raging in the abyss, "reached for the unattainable light"—but in vain. The demon who committed his monstrous deeds down there in the bottomless depths is none other than the subject who inserts meaning. It is the subject who strives to render familiar the alien world by "inserting" expressive power into it.

In Adorno's description it seems to be a stroke of good fortune when one manages to leave this abyss and reach the surrounding landscape, because it is only in this landscape, Adorno tells us, that we become aware of the light that the zealous hand has unsuccessfully striven to reach. One year after Adorno's visit to Naples, Sohn-Rethel recorded an evocative description of this moment: "Moonlit spikes rose up in the cool, silvery green glow of the jagged rocks bordering the outer crater. For a long time I couldn't tear myself away from the overwhelming beauty of this astronomical landscape, which seemed to acknowledge only the faded colors of the gemstones."[18]

But this beauty is not an end unto itself. The exceptional light illuminates the "truth": it is the abyss and the narrative of how it got to be so. The landscape, which arose as a result of the eruption, frames this gaping hole; we would know nothing about it without the "mighty stillness" of the "contour" of this landscape. It is the constellation circling around the crater—which is why the monstrous subject is mentioned only in the past tense; the constellation becomes possible only once the dialectical image produced by the subject has been exploded. And it is only by means of the constellation that we know—after its destruction—of the existence of the dialectical image.

This is why the landscape of the constellation has so little of its own to offer, and this is why it merely makes manifest the "demonic image" of the abyss. It marks the abyss by encircling it. For Adorno, the constellation is part and parcel of the dialectical image; it completes the dialectical image by destroying it.

Now it finally becomes clear what is meant by the "truth" of the Schubertian landscape, and what Vesuvius has to do with Schubert. The mechanism of the dialectical image and constellation is revealed, and this mechanism itself is what led to the revelation of the underlying truth in the first place. The bursting apart and constellation of the landscape of Schubert's music by means of the dialectical image of the potpourris leads to nothing more—but also to nothing less—than to insight about the truth of the dialectical image and constellation. Adorno had discovered an illustration of his evolving theory at the edge of the Vesuvius crater. A volcano is the purest conceivable form of porosity: one single hole with its border. Adorno shifted Benjamin and Lacis's social structure to a spectacle of nature, and in doing so returned to the origin of this structure. The stone on this site—which was porous because it was igneous rock—had been the starting point for identifying porosity in the essay on Naples.

Adorno landed on a powerful image for his concept of natural history when he determined that the apparently hellish, primeval landscape was actually the ruins of bourgeois culture burst asunder. "The ground (about eleven hundred meters above sea level) displays the manifold forms of cooled lava and scoriaceous residue,"[19] the Baedeker guide informs readers. Sohn-Rethel's description is more compelling: "The lava had congealed in the forms of human limbs, snakes of all sizes and coils, crocodiles, and other smooth, hairless bodies, truly like infernal entrails."[20] Here he was echoing Kracauer's use of the word "entrails" in describing Clavel's tower.[21]

That was it? That's all there was to it? Was Adorno really telling us that this was the truth of Schubert's music? A purely formal mechanism composed of something that is somehow demonic, and a structural idea that is set against this demonic element, but only in order to bring out that element more distinctly? Couldn't we have expected Adorno to supply us with critical tools for a socially and politically relevant analysis of the works of Schubert (and of Alban Berg)?

It is this disappointment that every reader of Adorno is bound to experience at least subconsciously: fired up by Adorno's analyses, they have to face the fact that the only practical consequence was a hallucinatory, circular textual progression. But this disappointment is unwarranted. Adorno was not actually retreating from societal criticism; he was digging deep into it. His model does not describe specific forms of ideology, but rather the conditions that allow for ideology in the first place. The dialectical image is the basic matrix for ideology; it arises from a misapprehension of the state of the world. Deciphering dialectical images facilitates a diagnosis of the ideologization; the destruction of the images on the path to the constellation marks at the least the prospect of a society free of ideology.

Adorno turned a method of composition into a utopian praxis and developed a materialism of aesthetic form, which, in turn, is largely responsible for the great fascination that his texts engender. The interlacing of the constellation and the explosion that culminates in it, the interlacing of continuous circling and suspense-packed narration, is a major feature of the texts' strong suggestiveness.

The Schubert essay, for example, encircles the abyss, then descends into hell. The encounter with the "demonic" doppelgänger, a self-recognition of the "sinking soul" as "inescapably trapped in the nexus of nature," makes it possible to blast apart subjective demonism and lead to the crater with which the essay opened. This circular progression in the essay consists of three sections, each of which itself encircles the abyss, and in this act of encircling recounts how the encircling was made possible. Adorno was follow-

VESUVIO (22) — IL PICCOLO CONO NEL GRAN CRATERE.

Eruption cone of Mount Vesuvius.

ing through with Hegel's idea of the design of an overall system as a circle composed entirely of circles—a "circle of circles."[22]

The "little" walks around the crater in the Schubert essay are dramatized in a variety of ways. In the third section Adorno allows for a bit of a climax to the account, with its sharpest depiction of the abyss, and the prospect of deliverance furnishes a true endpoint for the essay, though even the first section goes beyond the introductory establishment of the volcano image to introduce an explosive element: Romanticism's wrong-minded reception of Schubert left "hollow spaces in the [music's] erupted subjectivity."[23]

As was evident in the middle section of the *Wozzeck* essay, the second section here[24]—the middle circle—is closest to the center, and circumnavigated by the circular motion of the essay as a whole. After the destruction of the postcard landscape in the encounter with the demonic doppel-

gänger, the structure of the object under investigation becomes a programmatic one: Schubert's music is addressed
as the aforementioned "eccentric structure of this landscape, in which every point is equidistant from the center."[25]
As in the *Wozzeck* essay, the analysis of the musical material is situated primarily in the middle circle. In fine-tuning
his circular movement, Adorno shifts the contrast between
expressive and passive subject—which, at the beginning of
the essay, is distinguished by the different manners of death
into the form of Schubert's music itself—thus wresting from
this music what is most characteristic. Schubert, too, has a
"zealous hand" striving for totality, an "abstract will for pure
immanence of form,"[26] and, we are told, "Invention wields
constructive power to penetrate [the essence of the objectivities of form] emanating from the subject." At the same time,
however, holes are poked in these objectivities of form, such
as in the sonata form, straight into "the structure of subjective intentions," and thus in the middle of this constellation
its form is substantiated in the collapse of the "assertion of
the subject" and the explosive destruction of this subject's
inspirations.

So this was the development of the stylistic ideal that
Adorno announced to Berg after his stay in Naples: a tracing
of the constellation's equivalence and simultaneity, but one
that tells the dramatic story of how this simultaneity came
into being.

12

Snakelike Entrails

In September 1925, four young manic readers met up somewhere in Naples. They were all just learning to use the surface of their surroundings to analyze the world around them and to discern how a better one might be created. Kracauer and Adorno wrote about the demons in Positano, the intarsia woodwork in Sorrento, and the strange, eerie sea creatures. These were the images of the Kierkegaardian, personal inwardness that they sought to set against the seductive concepts of a new communal rhythm, against the porous entwinement that Sohn-Rethel tried to reformulate from Marx and that Benjamin had learned from Asja Lacis as a lesson in calling for a communist future. They wrestled with one another, the one employing an incendiary diction and the other putting on a show of impudence to compensate for his comparative youth.

While the four young intellectuals were getting together to wage a philosophical battle among affable adversaries, a battle that would culminate in their development of a sociological, literary, and epistemological utopia, another, decidedly unphilosophical battle had long since been decided.

"He does not look like the heartthrob you see on postcards," Benjamin wrote about Mussolini in September 1924; instead, he came across as "shady, shiftless, and arrogant, as though smeared in copious amounts of rancid oil. His body is as coarse and shapeless as a fat huckster's fist."[1]

While in Naples in 1922, Mussolini had made it clear that he intended to assume the office of prime minister, a goal he achieved by staging a "March on Rome." When Benjamin recorded his impression of Mussolini, the latter was struggling for power, hampered by his obvious involvement in political murders. But by the next year, when the four critical theorists gathered together, Mussolini had prevailed. European fascism had begun its triumphal march.

Kracauer was the only one of the critical theorists to broach the threat of fascism in his writing. Although Clavel is ever so briefly the revolutionary who wrests hollows from the water sprite in Kracauer's "Rocky Delusions in Positano," the essay as a whole focuses squarely on Clavel's demonic nature. At the time of Kracauer's and Adorno's visit, Clavel had been blasting for seventeen years, and there was no end in sight.

Clavel provided the critical theorists with the perfect project to think with, alongside the architecture of Naples, and for Kracauer, Clavel and his project were ripe subjects for interpretation. Kracauer had studied architecture, so it was no coincidence that at the Amalfi Coast he was most excited by odd housing projects. Additionally, the construction of and living in houses is a central metaphor in the texts of the critical theorists. The porosity of Naples was a constructional and architectural category. Most of the texts on Naples written by Adorno and his fellow critical theorists gravitated to the question of domestic living arrangements as a major contrast between their familiar setup in northern Europe and the bewildering south. Sohn-Rethel's "Ideal of the Broken-Down" begins with a description of Naples doors, which were always open. Door handles were pointless mythical entities, because doors were intended only to stay open. If a draft should nevertheless happen to slam them shut, people hastened to reopen them "while shrieking in horror and trembling all over their bodies": "Naples with closed doors would be like Berlin without rooftops."[2] Benjamin and Lacis refer to the "gloomy box of the Nordic house" as something utterly alien to Neapolitans: "each private attitude or act is permeated by streams of communal life. To exist, for the Northern European the most private of affairs, is here, as in the kraal, a collective matter. So the house is far less the refuge into which people retreat than the inexhaustible reservoir from which they flood out." The very notion of domestic living arrangements is subject to the overarching process of porous interpenetration: "Here, too, there is interpenetration of day and night, noise and peace, outer light and inner darkness, street and home." Bloch wrote, "one's residence partakes of the outdoors and is likewise a combination of interior and public sphere."[3]

When it comes to private space, the critic's task is to break down the contrast between private residence and public space and bring the Neapolitan collapse of this distinction right into one's living space, thus breaking apart the "gloomy box of the Nordic house" from within. Benjamin's *One-Way Street* had shown how: by situating Lukács's charnel house in chintzy bourgeoisie interiors. For him, the "soulless luxuriance" of interior design "becomes true comfort only in the presence of a dead body": "The bourgeois interior of the 1860s to the 1890s, with its gigantic sideboards distended with carvings, the sunless corners where palms sit, the balcony embattled behind its balustrade, and the long corridors with their singing gas flames, fittingly houses only the corpse. 'On this sofa the aunt cannot but be murdered.'"[4]

But for Kracauer, Clavel's project could also be a portent of death. Kracauer noted that the face of a Prussian builder who assisted with the blasting had come to resemble a Neapolitan, and he was bound to die here: "People explode here as well, because the end is never reached."[5] Kracauer wrote this pessimistic remark in reference to Clavel's battle against the demonic water; Clavel's battles against nature, Kracauer felt, had made him into a demon. "Clavel might regard himself as free [of nature], but it will ultimately overpower him."[6]

Clavel could be portrayed as a hero who wrested a fascinating life project from his illnesses and a hostile nature, but for the most part, he was viewed in harsher terms. Norman Douglas, a British Capri enthusiast, described Clavel as a deformed young Swiss man "with pushful and almost offensive manners, unhealthy complexion, and a horrible, rasping voice."[7] Clavel's physical appearance made people regard him as a creature who was not quite of this world. In the words of one obituary: "The Italians . . . regarded him as a demon, called him diabolo rosso, feared him as a sorcerer, and loved him as a bringer of luck. They secretly touched his body."[8]

Clavel certainly worked on his image. He wielded it as an intimidation tactic in disputes about the site of the tower. His many physical afflictions included a lack of one testicle, which, he claimed, his mother kept in a preserving jar.[9] He exploited even this flaw for his project of self-projection. Of a grotto that he blasted into the rocks, in which he planned to have concerts, he declared, "I turn to stone in this basic form—without anyone noticing—nature having taken the most vital thing from me."[10]

Kracauer inferred Clavel's demonic nature from the way the tower was set up, which, he claimed, "anticipated con-

structivism, unadorned and crystalline, but only super-
ficially related to the Bauhaus. For it is rage that lurks behind the form, stabbing berserkly into the void. The bed is
movable, like the one in the fairy tale that is meant to make
our skin crawl. The library shelves turn round and round,
and the modern registrar is encapsulated in an alcove from
which he may pop out satanically."[11] Clavel himself would
likely have agreed with this interpretation; he regarded
his building efforts as more tellurian than enlightening. It
took quite a while for Clavel to take notice of the theories
of Johann Jakob Bachofen, who also hailed from Basel, but
once he did, he wasted no time in laying claim to Bachofen's
mythically infused matriarchal morphology and calling the
tower an "architecture of the chthonic."[12] But for Kracauer,
Clavel's strange appearance was only a superficial matter,
and the chamber of horrors in which he resided was a mere
symptom. The reason for his demonic nature lay elsewhere.
Clavel became a demon because he lost all sense of proportion. The hollows, conceived of as a porous contrast to
the monstrous gelatinous creatures, took on a monstrous,
unwieldy, irrational structure all their own. "No one can
cope with the topography of this venation, which you crawl
through for two hours, uncertain still as to whether you've
seen even half of the openings. . . . The flights of stairs are
unfathomable, snakelike entrails slinking into the rooms."[13]

The journal *Berliner Illustrirte* pointed out that without a
guide, people would be unable to find their way out of this
"labyrinth of corridors."[14] In the Naples aquarium, Kracauer
was fascinated by porosity, tubular systems, and geometric patterns, which reminded him of the venation in Clavel's
tower. For Kracauer, the porous becomes the demonic element against which it was the strongest weapon for Adorno.

In making this shift, Clavel became the prototype for the momentous assertion of subsequent critical theory: that fascism was no accident of history, impelled by demonic barbarians, but could instead be explained as a consequence of an Enlightenment run amok. But was there a theoretical basis for this shift?

In addition to Adorno and Kracauer, Sohn-Rethel and his Russian schoolmate, and Benjamin and Lacis, there were two more friends who fired each other up with their readings and exchanges: Max Horkheimer and Friedrich Pollock. Shortly after they met in Frankfurt at the age of fifteen and sixteen, Horkheimer regarded Pollock as a co-conspirator in emancipating himself from his family home. They, too, had their Capri—without even going there. The *île heureuse* was (and remained) their locus of longing, envisioned expressionistically. Of all the avid reading groups associated with critical theory, Horkheimer and Pollock's was the stablest. The two of them entered into a friendship pact early on, as a model of and nucleus for "the creation of the solidarity of all people,"[15] and this pact—reevaluated from time to time— held them together until Pollock's death.

In 1994, Rolf Wiggershaus would write an essay about Pollock as the "last unknown" of the Frankfurt School. Pollock remains stuck in the role of "the man in the background,"[16] when compared with Adorno, Horkheimer, Marcuse, Fromm, and even Löwenthal, who has also remained relatively unknown. Pollock merits respect for putting aside his own ambition to promote the larger cause. He expressed resentment-free approval of Adorno's having taken over the role of Horkheimer's partner-in-theory by the time Adorno was in Los Angeles: "Only under your immediate supervision can [Adorno's] productive force become fruitful for our work."[17]

But Pollock's contribution to critical theory has now been acknowledged.[18] Adorno's purview was music, Löwenthal's literature, Horkheimer's the readjustment of the concept of theory itself, and Pollock's the economy. In the 1932 inaugural volume of the *Zeitschrift für Sozialforschung,* Pollock's essay, bearing the title: "The Current State of Capitalism and the Prospects for a Reorganization of the Planned Economy," immediately followed Horkheimer's programmatic introductory remarks. At this time it was still possible to envision getting beyond the capitalist economic order. Pollock walked his readers through the ways in which monopolistic tendencies could be regarded as a stage on the path to a planned economy, and he rejected market-conforming argumentation that deemed it impossible.

Still, this optimism could not be sustained once fascism had taken hold and they were forced to emigrate; instead, they suspected that the new rulers had succeeded in appropriating the drift of the planned economy and exploiting it for their own purposes. Pollock reacted to this development with his theory that "the monopolistic phase of capitalism liquidates the sphere of circulation, and increases capitalism's capacity to get its crises under control through planning," as Manfred Gangl notes.[19]

The new monopolistic economic system wasn't a consistent intensification of liberal capitalism and hence not a new—albeit disastrous—stage on the path to its collapse. Instead, Pollock assumed a coup de main-style takeover that dashed any hope of the self-destructive forces of capitalism. "But planned economy and state interventionism, which initially seemed to contain a promise of socialism, changed, and in the end stood for the opposite of the original hopes," Wiggershaus has written.[20]

The schematism that Pollock used in his reflections, and the precedence of economic analysis over political assessment, led to misunderstandings and intense discussions within the institute. In 1941, Adorno would complain to Horkheimer during the preparations for the programmatic "State Capitalism" issue of the *Zeitschrift für Sozialforschung* about Pollock's undialectical approach,[21] because Pollock's essay for this issue described what happens when the planned economy does not replace capitalism but instead is used by rulers to pacify it. Society no longer creates itself by a play of economic forces. The primacy of the economy is replaced by that of politics. In liberal capitalism the power structures had been created quasi-blindly through various actions by the social actors. Now, however, this power was plainly evident and enforced by the governing authorities with the tools of bureaucracy and administration.

Adorno and Horkheimer were initially displeased by this diagnosis because it destroyed any hope for the revolutionary escalation of the internal contradictions.[22] But it took the adoption of this diagnosis to enable them to create the matrix they could use to write *Dialectic of Enlightenment*. Gangl was right in claiming, "This is where Critical Theory in the strict sense truly began."[23]

Still, Adorno had already integrated this diagnosis underlying the argumentative level into the structure of his constellation back in 1936. Earlier on, it had been a strange variant of a Marxist theory of collapse. The productive forces would lead to a humane state of affairs, if the bourgeois subjects did not constrain those forces in the process of insertion. But this very constraint brings about an encounter with one's own demon and bursts apart constrictive subjectivity. This act of bursting the constellation preserves, in however reduced a form, the messianic element that Adorno secularized as the hope for a humane state of affairs.

But what would happen if this very change were transformed into its opposite, if, in accordance with Pollock's diagnosis, the end of the liberal era were not its consequential collapse but instead its usurpation by monopoly capitalism? Later, in *Minima Moralia,* Adorno would claim that this failure had begun quite early, with the stabilization of the German currency,[24] that is, with the introduction of the Rentenmark in 1923. According to Adorno, this development put an end to the chaos that in the logic of the collapse theory would have triggered the breakdown of the capitalist system. His assessment accords with Sohn-Rethel's description of the last years of inflation, which provided a clear reference to the chaos that was then eliminated: "You cannot imagine how the world looked, how everyday life played out, in this final stage of inflation, where no boundary whatever could be drawn between civilian life and criminality. It was a field of adventures, this city. Nothing went its normal way. I later experienced that once again in Naples."[25]

In his theoretical musings, Adorno furnished an audacious reaction to that limination of the chaos liberal era: the model of the constellation remains intact. But it is usurped by the monopolistic era. And in the description of this usurpation it retains its value as a diagnosis of society. The first essay that brought this theoretical sleight of hand to the fore was arguably Adorno's most notorious one: "On Jazz." In this essay, Adorno criticized jazz music so savagely that even Kracauer was taken aback and urged him to tone it down. The rhetorical lengths to which Adorno went in ascribing fascist tendencies to jazz even though the German fascists actually banned jazz makes the essay an easy target for mockery and alarm. The ascetic Kant's definition of marriage ("the union of two persons of different sexes for lifelong possession of each other's sexual attributes"),[26] and elitist twelve-tone specialist Adorno's criticism of jazz, both rank high in the list of the most blatant examples of quixotic philosophizing.[27] But no matter how apt any condemnations of Adorno's text may be, the following chapter will show how a new era in Adorno's theory was taking shape. In the essay on jazz, Adorno was dipping his toe into the waters of depicting the structure of the constellation as an appropriated one.

13
The Treasureless Trove
of the Functioning

Tiberius is effectively the patron saint of the island of Capri. Benjamin invoked his name to justify his own inability to leave the island. Savinio's travel account recorded the long distances he traveled as he followed the traces of the omnipresent spirit of Tiberius. But just two generations after Tiberius's death, a hostile and tendentious historiography had begun to denigrate him as a dirty old man. Tiberius is alleged to have gone to Capri in order to indulge uninhibitedly in his perverse tendencies, directed principally at young boys. This image of unconstrained sexuality could easily be invoked again when the Blue Grotto was discovered. In hailing this discovery, Gregorovius depicted the site as the "island of the gruesome debauchee Tiberius."[1]

Nonconformism, which had such a strong appeal for artists and others who fancied themselves part of bohemian society, also had a sexual dimension. An escape from the narrow confines of one's home was often also an escape from conventional notions of sexuality in which same-sex love had no place. From the start, the early nineteenth-century German poet and dramatist August von Platen associated the fishermen's archetypal masculinity with homosexual proclivities. The practice—dating back to when people first began to swim in the newly discovered grotto—of hav-

ing a boy dive down for coins, accorded well with this image: "The image of the young, naked male body whose alluring contours are mirrored in the heavenly silvery blue of the
water has been a key fascinating aspect of the Blue Grotto
for generations."[2] Fantasies of unbridled or perverse sexuality taking place within villa walls have drawn people to Capri since the days of Tiberius. A recent travel guide contin-
ues to depict Capri's "wild years"—from 1820 to 1930—with
an unmistakable undertone of indignation: "And those who
were drawn to it often regarded Capri as a refuge, where
they could escape the parochial bourgeois moral codes and
social constraints back home and could consequently carry
on however they pleased, more often than not showing little
regard for the people of Capri."[3] It follows up this commentary by listing a couple of the usual suspects, among them
Baron Jacques d'Adelswärd-Fersen, who, because he staged
tableaux vivants, living pictures featuring young men, which
drew on ancient lore, had already suffered severe repercus-
sions (suicide attempt and entering the Foreign Legion after
being convicted in Paris) before heading to Capri, where he
resumed staging living pictures.[4] Friedrich Alfred Krupp's
death in 1902 may have been a suicide, after he was anon-
ymously "accused of homosexual and pedophile activities"
in Capri.[5]

Uninhibited and purportedly deviant sexuality is, however, not only an import of those who followed in the footsteps of August Kopisch and Platen; Nordic guests have always ascribed wanton sexuality to Naples, portraying it as
a den of iniquity. Among the many colorful attractions that
Gregorovius enumerated during his visit to Naples were the
"loose girls" who embark on "their amorous adventures
quite ominously over a glass of sulfur water."[6] In 1834, during

his stay in Naples and the surrounding area, Hans Christian Andersen confided to his diary: "My blood is in strong motion. Enormous sensuality and struggle against myself. If it is really a sin to satisfy this mighty lust, then I will fight against it. I am still innocent, but my blood burns. In dreams all my innards boil."[7] In 1851, Gustave Flaubert pinned the blame on Vesuvius for boosting his libido: "Here in mellow Partenopeia [i.e., Naples] I am perpetually tumescent. I fuck like a donkey on the loose. Even the pressure of my trousers provokes an erection. One of these days I shall even condescend to impale the washerwoman who thinks that I am 'molto gentile.' It is perhaps the proximity of Vesuvius which is overheating my loins."[8] Axel Munthe regarded the libidinous atmosphere that prevailed in Naples as the complement to the rampage of death. Reflecting on the cholera epidemic in 1884, he wrote:

> Wherever this equilibrium is upset by some accidental
> cause, be it pestilence, earthquake or war, vigilant Nature
> sets to work at once to readjust the balance, to call forth
> new beings to take the place of the fallen. Compelled by
> the irresistible force of a Natural Law men and women fall
> in each other's arms blindfolded by lust, unaware that it is
> Death who presides over their mating, his aphrodisiac in
> one hand, his narcotic in the other.[9]

Lacis and Benjamin's Naples text opens with a priest's indecent offenses (which in the typescript are labeled as "sodomitic") and culminates in a brief hint of erotic peril.[10] Noting the way Neapolitans speak with their hands, their fingers engaging their bodies in the process, the authors remark: "These configurations return to their fastidiously specialized eroticism."[11] A stranger is sent away in an act of compassion or even humanitarianism to safeguard that stranger from being sold down the river.

Sexuality is the theme of Adorno's essay on jazz. Not only the theme: sexuality turns out to be the "truth" of jazz, sexuality should be the result of the constellation that the essay is trying to bring about. Everything comes down to the physical empiricism of sexuality, to the "concrete historically determined constellation of social identities and sexual energy," as Adorno writes.[12] But this time, unlike in the earlier essays, the construction of the constellation fails. Let's examine how the essay stages this failure.

Adorno defines the object of his investigation, "jazz," in this way as closure of the mechanism of the dialectical image that is rendered in a particular sound. This jazz sound is not bound to any one compositional style or instrument; it is defined by its function, by the possibility of letting the rigid vibrate, or more generally, "by the opportunity to produce interferences between the rigid and the excessive."[13] The positions are clearly assigned: The rigid element is the society, and the vibrating or excessive element is the subject that that seeks to confront—or flee—this society. In Adorno's earlier conception the subject has inserted subjective expression into rigid things and in doing so created what appears to be a second nature. Now the agent of this insertion is society, the second nature that is already in place. Everything is rigid and the subject is used to create the appearance of vibration. Earlier on, the subject's insertion of meaning had initiated a process that wound up being larger than itself. Now the process of insertion is a trick of the rigid society, and the automatism leading to the constellation has come to a halt—the jazz vibrato is "merely inserted into the rigid sound, and syncopation into the basic meter," as Adorno writes.[14]

This vibrato is played out in all possible aspects of jazz, while the individual sections adhere to a single principle. What appears to be the "vibrating" element—that is, the socially progressive, utopian aspect—is exposed, in each individual step, as something *merely* inserted. In the first section after the introduction this is the immediate utility of jazz. In accordance with the principle of vibrato, its objectivity is "no more than a pasted-on ornament meant to deceive us about the extent to which it is merely an object."[15] Adorno likewise deciphered as deceptive the impression that it is a genuinely democratic form of music: "Its attitude of immediacy, which can be defined in terms of a rigid system of tricks, is deceptive when it comes down to class differences."[16] The purported possibility of a plebiscitary reception is also "all mere decorum: the only melodies that find their way into the public memory are the melodies which are the most easily understood and the most rhythmically trivial."[17]

The irrationality of success and failure of jazz pieces might fuel the hope that no system of any kind influences it. But according to Adorno, this irrationality is only the destructive kind that inheres in the system anyway. And the terms that serve to reframe this chaos as a creative one— "inspiration, the concept of genius, creativity,"[18] and so forth—are mere "depraved magical formulations" that are used for the vibrato. The following two sections of the essay show the origin of this vibrato in Adorno's philosophy by laying bare the supposed originality of jazz as modern repression in disguise,[19] and by revealing the law of the market that something "must constantly remain the same while at the same time constantly simulating the 'new.'"[20] In both instances we see the dialectical image of history at work, with something seemingly new inserted into what is unchanging and the new assuming the countenance of the seemingly ancient.

But perhaps the societal innovation of jazz comes down to the fact that the composition itself is not really the decisive element, that its aesthetic effect lies instead in *re*production, in the virtuosity of the arranger or the performance, just as the Neapolitans once made a practice of disregarding objects' intended uses, instead reappropriating them for their constellations. Here, too, Adorno claims, the mechanism of the inoperative dialectical image applies; here, too, the process of insertion gets co-opted: "The stimulation and the artistic piece, the new color and the new rhythm are merely inserted along with the banal—just as the jazz vibrato is inserted into the rigid sound, and syncopation in the basic meter. This element of interference in jazz is accomplished by the arrangement of the composition."[21] But surely, then, at least the distribution of labor is exemplary for future aesthetic processes of production? No, Adorno insists, it is not, because it, too, is a romanticization "in the sense of a vague 'avant-garde' quality, in the sense of the 'tempo of the times.'"[22]

With the amateur, the jazz industry draws the naive audience into the production process. To avoid pure dilettantism, it requires specialists for the additional production steps, which are camouflaged as a progressive distribution of labor. In the next section, the nature of the amateur is revealed as "the subjective correlative of an objective formal structure,"[23] which was established as the core structure of jazz:

> The helplessness of the person who is excluded from
> the specialized trade, who experiences the same fear
> in the face of music, evinces something akin to fear as
> if it were a social power and, because of his fear, aspires
> to adapt himself to it, without, however, succeeding at
> it—this helplessness is just as important an ingredient
> [in its success] as the educated mundane consciousness
> of the habitué. After all, the two belong together as
> the constitutive elements of jazz: helplessness (the
> whimpering vibrato) and the average consciousness
> (banality).[24]

At the other end of the spectrum, Adorno concludes that things don't look much better with regard to the sophistication level of taste in jazz; here, too, vibrato is only an instrument for the rigid society to appear less rigid: "But the individual element which is inserted into jazz . . . does not generate or have control over itself. It has become rigid, formulaic, spent—the individual elements are now in just the same position as social convention was previously."[25]

In the following section, the purely tonal, physical model widens out to stylistic concepts; the phenomenon of interference between life and rigidity is allocated to salon and march music.[26] Adorno positions the treatment of the gait in jazz in the space between salon and march music. Surprisingly, a brief moment of genuine bourgeois emancipation ensues. Dance is demythologized as a bourgeois gait, as it might have occurred in the salons in the habitus of the class's newly found self-awareness. But before this gait is in turn transposed into a "new magic,"[27] which is to say, rhythmically-based marching—so before the "vibration" of the gait also proves to be rigid—Adorno wished to linger briefly on its emancipatory potential.

Here there is, once again, a spark of the possibility of a constellation and the attendant utopian content. For a brief moment, the new form of art seems capable of bringing expression to the "physical empirical realm of regulated-arbitrary life."[28] Adorno describes film scenes of this arbitrary life, with people strolling along the beach, a woman busying herself with her shoe, and jazz music always works so well with it that it no longer stands out.

So is jazz ultimately the expression of a contemporary nonchalance, an emancipation of the class that falls somewhere between the Neapolitan proletariat and the bourgeoisie wrestling forlornly with itself? An emancipation that is also sexual: Adorno can simply reenvision all these random moments of everyday life as sexual innuendos.

And now, finally, after a blank line, jazz, like Benjamin and Lacis's Naples, is established as an "arena" for a "concrete historically determined constellation of social identities and sexual energy."[29] Everything presses on to the scene of a self-encounter. The dialectical image, which could function as a doppelgänger, has been examined in great detail. Naturally it is the vibrato, this time as personified syncopation. In departing from the beat, "individual contingency is embodied."

But it turns out that Adorno trusts the contingency that has been attained at long last to only "a very minor degree."[30] And the emancipatory hope for jazz only lasts a brief and dramatic but futile moment, because here, too, the process that leads to the constellation comes to a standstill. The power relations are clearly distributed. Earlier on, the subject could shudder and draw back at this sight of his doppelgänger. Now the subject is himself the dialectical image. The society with which it is confronted uses the process of insertion for its own ends, and doesn't care one bit that it faces a representation of its second nature. In this way, Adorno argues, the jazz subject lends this higher authority "expression without softening it by this expression."[31]

Part of the charm of Naples was its perpetual broken-ness; people could blithely ignore the dictates of technology and reappropriate strictures imposed by modernity. "Technology does not actually begin until man vetoes the inimical and sealed off automatism of machines and steps into their world himself,"[32] Sohn-Rethel wrote in his essay "The Ideal of the Broken-Down." He also insisted, "Mechanisms cannot function as the civilizing continuum they were designed for here: Naples turns its back on them."[33]

One mark of the new monopolistically governed world was that everything worked far too well and no subversion of the "automatisms of machines" was possible. Where could used-up, outdated material for the constellation be obtained? Broken objects, once an ideal for Sohn-Rethel and others, had been brought to the repair shop for a thorough overhaul. In 1934, when Adorno made Oxford the first stage of his immigration, the imagery for trouble-free equipment was already in place. His uncle Bernhard Wingfield had founded the Power Plant Company there, a factory that specialized in turbine blades. In *Minima Moralia,* Adorno recalled English acquaintances bringing him children's books, and the foreignness of the language he had yet to grasp conjured up a particular image in his mind: "The peculiar inaccessibility of the books, with their glaring pictures, titles, and vignettes, and their indecipherable text, filled me with the belief that in general, objects of this kind were not books at all, but advertisements, perhaps for machines like those my uncle produced in his London factory."[34]

In Adorno's conceptual world, this machinery is linked with sexuality—which should actually have become visible as a corporeal concretion at the end of the essay on jazz— and creates a monster. In this essay, the jazz orchestra mutates into a machine with a "double function" once it has recounted the story of the usurpation of the constellation right down to the scene with the self-encounter, the double function being "that of the menacingly unleashed castration machine and again of the persistently pounding, potent copulation machine."[35]

Horkheimer, who thought highly of the essay as a whole, suggested a few deletions in the course of the revisions, particularly in regard to the passages on sexuality. Horkheimer was worried that the New York "society analysts" would read these passages against the backdrop of a theoretical socialization, which would lead to misunderstandings.[36] Adorno fought these deletions vehemently, appealing to the group's "shared intellectual responsibility."[37] In his eyes, the essay was composed with this machine as its climax. The connection between syncopation and the fear of castration is not an associative one, he argues; syncopation is one of the many dialectical images that originate in an act of insertion, constituting a "historical concretion" and "the fear of castration as a phenomenon."[38] The double machine is not some sort of crazed fantasy of an intellectual who had not sufficiently absorbed his readings of Freud or Wilhelm Reich. For Adorno, the machine (which didn't make it into the published essay despite Adorno's adamant defense of its inclusion) is in "physical" view.[39]

The elimination of the copulation machine works to the detriment of an essay that aims at a constellation of sexuality and seeks to present a distorted picture, but this loss does not take away from the constant production of dialectical images. The final section introduces another machine that is arguably even worse than the castration and copulation machine, namely the "unbearable Wurlitzer organ,"[40] which, according to Adorno, encapsulates every dreadful characteristic of vibrato—that is, mere "embellishment": "In it, the charater of the jazz vibrato comes definitively to the fore."[41]

So in the end, something is once again uncovered. But this staging of truth is an amputated one. Earlier on, the mechanism by which something could be revealed with the constellation had indeed been revealed. Now, this mechanism was stalled; it was used by monopolism to bring the constellation to a halt, whereupon the only thing left to do was to produce continual images of this halting, revealing the illusion of the monstrous machines that supposedly set things in motion, while actually holding them rigid. This problematic process highlights yet another characteristic of Adorno's texts, another component of the fascinating challenges they pose for readers. There were hallucinatory circles in the initial concept of the constellation in Adorno's texts, whereas now, with the change in the concept of the constellation, a relentless repetition has been added: we go from one dialectical image to the next without an arrival of the constellation; it is a sustained, unending horror, a mill wheel of hopelessness.

14

Parthenope Washes Ashore

A boat ride from Capri to Positano takes the traveler past a picturesque archipelago, Li Galli, which is located right in front of Clavel's tower. His brother René wanted to buy the largest of the three islands,[1] but in 1922 the Russian dancer and choreographer Léonide Massine beat him to it. Real estate ownership comes with obligations, and Massine had some ideas in mind. Gilbert Clavel reported, "He plans to construct a huge building on the 'Isola Lunga,' twenty meters long and fourteen meters wide (not a good proportion). I did not have a clear idea of his project. He spoke about a Greek portico, all in marble (!), and a terrace he intends to use as a theater and dance school. A dance colony on the Sirenusas!"[2] None other than Le Corbusier later helped Massine with the renovations. Elizabeth Taylor is said to have offered Massine a million dollars in 1964, but to no avail.[3] In 1989, another world-famous dancer—Rudolf Nureyev—was able to acquire it for himself.

According to legend, however—as Clavel indicated by his use of the word *Sirenusas*—sirens inhabited the archipelago in the mythical past. La Capria informs us that this is squarely within the Homeric portion of the Gulf. After Odysseus used cunning tricks to get past the sirens, they hurled themselves into the sea.[4] Naples, which was once called Par-

thenope, originated when one of the sirens—Parthenope—
washed right up to Adorno's doorstep, you might say, as his
hotel was on Via Partenope, a street named for this siren.[5]

In the opening essay of Adorno and Horkheimer's *Dialectic of Enlightenment,* one of the most influential books in
the history of modern philosophy, the encounter with the
sirens serves as a culminating point in the history of civilization, and the authors devote an excursus to *The Odyssey.*
Readers first encountering this text can easily picture why it
electrified an entire generation. Even those who are initially
baffled by the work are likely to be impressed by its way of
laying out an all-encompassing history of mankind, written
at the moment of that history's greatest catastrophe. What
a stroke of luck it was that after years of aiming to work together, Horkheimer and Adorno finally seized the opportunity to merge their writing styles and achieve this product of
inexorable verve. They wrote *Dialectic of Enlightenment* together on the West Coast, about a twenty-minute drive west
of downtown Los Angeles, in an area that an ingenious re-
altor dubbed the "California Riviera." Its street names—San
Remo Drive, Monaco Drive—appealed to many European immigrants who associated these names with their dream des-
tinations. The resulting geographical hodgepodge also su-
perimposed a faux Gulf of Naples on the area. Napoli, Capri,
and Sorrento Drive intermingled with the southern French
network of roads, and Lion Feuchtwanger and Thomas
Mann lived on Amalfi Drive before moving into their villas (which today serve as scholarly residences). Hanns Eis-
ler, with whom Adorno wrote the book *Composing for Films*
(*Komposition für den Film*), also lived on Amalfi Drive, number 689.

"Max and I are now working extremely well together,"[6]

Adorno wrote to his parents in describing his work with Horkheimer on *Dialectic of Enlightenment*. For the most part, he told them, "We have discussions, come to an agreement, then formulate our text together, often with one of us starting a sentence and the other dictating it to the end, which is actually possible because what we want to say is always totally clear in advance."[7]

It was clear not only because they had discussed it in advance, but also because several variants of *Dialectic of Enlightenment* already existed. In Kracauer's mythical phantasmagoria of Positano, for example, there are several allusions to Odysseus.[8] For Kracauer, the route from Positano to the Neapolitan aquarium was Enlightenment in a nutshell. In the Fresco Hall, where visitors can admire Hans von Marées's *Allure of Life in the Sea and on the Beach* (*Reiz des Meeres- und Strandlebens*), the deep sea creatures that had to be imprisoned to make these kinds of idylls possible are right under their feet. The mythically infused demonic water that Clavel had had to blast his way through was now tamed in the aquarium. In "The Mass Ornament," Kracauer tells of man's struggle against nature in a manner that makes the essay a kind of *Dialectic of Enlightenment* avant la lettre.

The impeded constellation provides the framework for Adorno and Horkheimer's discussion. Once again, the stampede toward a constellation is staged, and in the process the expectation placed on it is heightened in the extreme. By situating the moment of the doppelgänger encounter at the beginning of human history, Adorno renders its repetition a true historical promise—a hope that will be dashed.

The dialectical image had the strategic benefit of making the subject focus on his own naturalness. From the horror of this status a transition needs to occur that would lead it to be more than just nature. Adorno projects this scene onto the historical moment at which something like subjectivity (and hence history) is first generated. The "complex concatenation of nature" is transcended in that moment, and nature becomes more than nature—and mankind opens its eyes.[9] The unfamiliar is greeted with a "cry of terror," as *mana.*"[10] But the ensuing shudder also enables the "idle" to transcend itself: "What is later called subjectivity, freeing itself from the blind anxiety of the shudder, is at the same time the shudder's own development; life in the subject is nothing but what shudders, the reaction to the total spell that transcends the spell."[11] The constitution of the human is the primordial form of transcendence by means of shuddering. Later, when this society, for which the subject is responsible, has become second nature, the shudder will be performed at the site of this very second nature.

Adorno's versatile little narrative had suddenly turned into the nucleus of human history. If his encounter with the self-made monster were to work, it would mark the moment at which the chaotic society became a decent and reasonable one. The first chapter of *Dialectic of Enlightenment,* "The Concept of Enlightenment," prepares the ground for initiating this moment. As in the essays on *Wozzeck* and Schubert, the chapter is divided into three sections,[12] and each closes with a scene of shuddering self-encounter. But as in the essay on jazz, the process leading to the constellation comes to a halt.

At the end of the third section we are finally given the good news that the shudder of the mana scene could be repeated in modern times with the possibility "to recognize power even within thought itself as unreconciled nature."[13]

The final sentence dashes the hope that a "remembrance of nature within the subject" might finally take place: "But in face of this possibility, enlightenment, in the service of the present, is turning itself into an outright deception of the masses."[14]

15
Blood Miracle in Little Italy

Once Adorno was in American exile, Naples seemed far away. Adorno's essay on jazz could be read as the final reference to the Neapolitan constellation at the moment it was rendered impossible.

But when Adorno arrived in the melting pot that was New York in February 1938, the city had long since copied a Neapolitan ritual. Back in 1925, Adorno was probably still traveling somewhere along the Amalfi Coast on September 19,[1] and so he missed the spectacle of the so-called blood miracle that took place on this day in Naples. But he had surely been told about this grand procession—along with so many other spectacles that struck northern Europeans as whimsical and peculiar—in which the statue of San Gennaro was carried to the cathedral, and about how intently and anxiously everyone waited to find out whether the blood stored in small ampoules of the archbishop and patron saint of Naples, who had been beheaded many centuries earlier, would liquefy this time around. If it didn't, the crowd, fearing the onset of catastrophes and misfortune, would break out into loud weeping.

In Little Italy in Manhattan, there are no ampoules of San Gennaro's blood, but when September 19 rolls around, Mulberry Street is transformed into a grand festival, and the familial relationship to the saints is fostered. "The old Italian lady who with devout simplicity consecrates a candle to St. Gennaro to protect her grandson in the war may be closer to the truth than the high priests and pontiffs who, untainted by idolatry, bless the weapons against which St. Gennaro is powerless,"[2] Adorno wrote in the "Elements of Anti-Semitism," another fragment in *Dialectic of Enlightenment.*

Flowing blood makes its way into Adorno's excursus on *The Odyssey* as well—not at some peripheral spot, but at one that leads straight into hell. We read this about Odysseus's encounter with his dead mother: "Sacrificial blood is required as a pledge of living memory before the shades can speak, breaking free, however vainly and ephemerally, from mythic muteness."[3] Blood rarely flows in Adorno's texts, as it carries connotations of racist identity politics.[4] Its appearance in such a positive context is astonishing—and for good measure as a sacrifice, which Adorno's excursus treats, in long passages, as a first deception of the Enlightenment thinker. So how can sacrificial blood possibly be integrated into Adorno's model of the constellation?

The brief description of Odysseus's encounter with the sirens in the opening essay of *Dialectic of Enlightenment* stands out among the book's many highlights. The heroically auto-aggressive act of the commander Odysseus, who ties himself up in order to hear the sirens singing without perishing in the process, who plugs up the ears of his rowers—the echo of the self-subjugation in the pallid pleasure of the modern concert-goer. Any reader unmoved by this page and a half of explication and annihilation of culture would have to be heartless.

But when it comes to the excursus—which comments on the entirety of *The Odyssey*—isn't this part a bit disappointing? Of course Adorno could not keep delivering the kind of pithy, dynamic surprises he had in the brief siren scene in "The Concept of Enlightenment," which invokes what is likely the best known episode of *The Odyssey*. And the commentator has every right to focus on the story of the return home and the marriage story instead of the adventure narrative. But is it reasonable to make the woman, as a "representative of nature," the first dialectical image we encounter in the excursus on *The Odyssey*?[5] Even if the suppression of passion that Adorno recounts in discussing the Circe stage of Odysseus's journey is part and parcel of the self-enchainment of the "prototypical bourgeois," isn't Adorno's personal history intruding a bit too much?

In the cultural milieu of California immigrants, Adorno's keen interest in female attractiveness resulted in a series of severe emotional upsets. In the spring of 1943, he came to grips with an unhappy affair he had had with the screenwriter Renée Nell, putting on a brave face in a letter to his parents: "And I'm living on, though with very little facility for abstinence (my writing on Homer is a critique of abstinence)."[6] As a result, following the dialectical image of "woman," marriage, in all its ambiguity, serves as an essential step on the path to determining the truth content of *The Odyssey*. "Undoubtedly, marriage forms part of the primal rock of myth at the base of civilization. But its mythic solidarity and permanence jut from myth, as the small island realm rises from the endless sea,"[7] Adorno wrote. He was likely aware that this passage had tipped too far into the personal arena, so the next section in the published version—which leads into hell—took a different tack.

In an earlier version, however, the island-realm metaphor of the married couple leads straight to the constellation that constitutes the truth of the odyssey, for below the staging of the failure of the constellation in the opening essay, Adorno's original structure is at work in full force in the Odysseus excursus.

In Adorno's interpretation, Homer lets details of his narrative grow so outsized that they compromise the narrative structure: "If it is true . . . that in Homer the similes acquire an autonomy vis-à-vis the content . . . then the same antagonism to the way language is constrained by the complex of intentions is expressed in them. Engrossed in its own meaning, the image developed in language becomes forgetful and pulls language itself into the image rather than making the image transparent and revealing the logical sense of the relationship."[8]

This is again the process of the dialectical image. The dead things, in which the meaning is inserted, are in this case the images of the metaphor. And as always in Adorno's dialectical images, "the force of the material goes beyond the intention of the metaphor."[9]

If Adorno wishes to constellate the truth about *The Odyssey,* he can employ Homer's metaphors. He did not insist on just any kind of metaphor, but rather on one that, for him, entails "the substance appearing in naked form as the story nears its end."[10] The passage in which the marriage is an island, a metaphor for the happiness of the reuniting spouses, goes on to say: "And as when the land appears welcome to men who are swimming, / after Poseidon has smashed their strong-built ship on the open / water, pounding it with the weight of wind and the heavy sea, . . . / . . . gladly they set foot on the shore, escaping the evil; / so welcome was her husband to her as she looked upon him, / and she could not let him go from the embrace of her white arms."[11]

In Adorno's view, the "bare substance" of the Homeric

epic that emerges in this vivid comparison is "an attempt to attend to the endlessly renewed beating of the sea on the rocky coast, and to patiently reproduce the way the water floods over the rocks and then streams back from them with a roar, leaving the solid ground glowing with deeper color."[12] A demonstrative set of images, the lowest common denominator, one might say, of what is truly at issue on the venturesome surface of the *Odyssey:* withstanding the many dangers posed by the sea and reaching the safety of land.[13] But Adorno employs this imagery of the plot to construct a metaphor for the manner in which the tale is told. Roaring, he says, is the sound of epic speech when it wishes to extract all that is rock-solid and particular, all that is worth telling, from all that is flowing, ambiguous, and interchangeable.

Adorno uses the technique of deciphering dialectically when he infers from Homer's linguistic images the way Homer designs his images. But Adorno also finds a model for this technique on the level of the narration itself, in one of the rare instances in which Odysseus can be considered a model, an instance where the underworld is the setting for deciphering the images.

It is not especially surprising, of course, that a descent into hell figures in an essay about *The Odyssey,* but Adorno makes the discussion of this descent the most significant and final stage of his essay (in *The Odyssey* it appears in the middle of the story).[14] At the end of a parade of phantoms of deceased companions, Odysseus's own mother appears to him. She, too, has died, so she can also be nothing but a phantom, a "phantom, like epic narrative at the moments when language gives way to images."[15] The administration, in doses, of sacrificial blood to the phantom is itself a parable for the skillful handling of dialectical images. They cannot be dismissed out of hand as irrational. Adorno is conciliatory toward the religious practice of the blood miracle because it doesn't abstract the substance of belief to the point of unrecognizability. He is also conciliatory in regard to the dialectical image, because only then can its truth content be extracted. However, this truth is again merely insight into deception, into the spectral nature of the image, into the fact of facing a dead person. The image of the mother who has come to life reveals its own nullity.[16]

16
The Prophecy of Positano

The *Dialectic of Enlightenment* was written in Brentwood, California, situated between downtown Los Angeles and the Pacific, where Adorno followed Horkheimer at the end of 1941 shortly before the United States entered the war. There, far away from the tedious work at the Institute for Social Research, they hoped to get the focus they needed for their book. At some point in 1942, while still working on *Dialectic of Enlightenment,* Adorno began a new notebook reserved for ideas and notes about Kafka. Ten years later he turned them into an essay. He outlined a thirteen-part "arrangement of the material,"[1] and labeled the individual notes with the numeral of the bullet point they would go with. Then, using this structure, he wrote the text in his notebook in virtually letter-perfect form. Once a note had made its way into the text, it was crossed out.

The matrix along which the notes were joined together to form a continuous text is, once again, that of the constellation. After an introductory section, the next section described the method he will use to approach the riddle that is "Kafka," a figure that has been subject to so many attempts at demystification. Adorno plans to listen closely to metaphors that free themselves from their intended use: "At times, words, metaphors in particular, detach themselves and achieve a certain autonomy."[2] In the third part, Kafka is revealed to be a master of the constellation, creating images out of the "rubbish of reality"; the fourth part provides an example, with the individuals constellated by gestures, revealing their alienation: "The crucial moment, however, toward which everything in Kafka is directed, is that in which men become aware that they are not themselves—that they themselves: are things."[3] In the fifth section it becomes apparent that Adorno's model is still operating on the transition from liberalism to monopoly capitalism. It is this transition that produces the refuse with which the image of the new epoch can be constellated: "Kafka unmasks monopolism by focusing on the waste-products of the liberal era that it liquidates."[4] In the sixth section this transition finally leads to hell. This section lays out the inner logic Adorno used to revitalize the model of the constellation, the failure of which he has impressively demonstrated in his essay on jazz.

During the writing process, Adorno dropped a few of the points in the original outline. Instead of thirteen points there were only now only nine. And point 7, which was originally in the center—titled "fascism prophesied" in one spot—slipped into point 6. In this section, which was no longer in the chronological midpoint yet continued to function as the essay's conceptual center, the hell in Adorno's model, the eerie landscape of Positano, finds a brutal counterpart in reality, namely in Auschwitz. After all, the hellish dialectical image, the "insertion" of apparent life even into death, is unsettlingly apt as a description of the tortures carried out by the Nazis in the concentration camps, as Adorno describes them in his essay on Kafka:

> Perhaps that is what is meant by the tale of Gracchus, the
> once wild hunter, a man of force who was unable to die.
> Just as the bourgeoisie failed to die. History becomes Hell
> in Kafka because the chance which might have saved was
> missed. This hell was inaugurated by the late bourgeoisie
> itself. In the concentration camps, the boundary between
> life and death was eradicated. A middle-ground was cre-
> ated, inhabited by living skeletons and putrefying bodies,
> victims unable to take their own lives, Satan's laughter at
> the hope of abolishing death. As in Kafka's twisted epics,
> what perished there was that which had provided the
> criterion of experience—life lived out to its end. Gracchus
> is the consummate refutation of the possibility banished
> from the world: to die after a long and full life.[5]

In the historical and philosophical construction of Critical
Theory, late capitalism devolved into National Socialism because the opportunity to bring about a radical change and
form a truly rational society was missed. Adorno's theory reacted with a claim that this radical change, the element that
might have "saved," namely the constellation, was usurped
by the Nazis, so now only demonic dialectical images were
produced without the "saving" that could have occurred had
the constellation been able to destroy these demonic elements. He integrated the Holocaust into his theory as the
most extreme manifestation of the dialectical image.

Someone emerges "from a rumbling, heaped up, cooling
crater into a painfully fine and filmy white light."[6] A colos-
sal catastrophe has ripped open the earth, a monster, deep
down in the crater, blasted through in a rage. But now it is
over. The person emerging from the crater can keep circling
the catastrophe at its edge to ensure that it is not forgotten.

"Infernal entrails" on Mount Vesuvius.

When Adorno returned to Germany in 1949, was he not repeating the path he had imagined more than twenty years earlier at the beginning of his Schubert essay? Adolf Hitler, a dictator who, like Clavel, lacked a testicle, had shattered the achievements of the Enlightenment and turned the world into hell. Adorno could now use his narrative to encircle the fact of the Holocaust and ensure that the abyss caused by the Holocaust would never be forgotten. Now the encounter with one's own demonic double is the encounter with the dialectical image of that which mankind is capable of. Terrified in the face of the human-made catastrophe, the postwar subject must prevent any forms of "coming to terms with the past" or "putting it all in perspective." In this way, Adorno's narrative became one of the key philosophical narratives for postwar Germany.

17
Afterlife

The mid-1920s were years "at the edge of time," as Hans Ulrich Gumbrecht called this period.[1] Lenin died, Bohr and Heisenberg threw the very foundations of physics into question, Hitler wrote *Mein Kampf,* Heidegger wrote *Being and Time,* Charlie Chaplin filmed *The Gold Rush,* and Eisenstein filmed *Battleship Potemkin.* During this period, which later turned out to be a dance on the volcano, four intellectuals at a sensitive juncture in their philosophical lives set off to spend time in close proximity to an actual volcano.

The Gulf of Naples had a major impact on their thinking. The experience of the city of Naples became an essential checkpoint for the analysis of modernity, and via the concept of the constellation urbanity opened new avenues to philosophical knowledge. The "Virgilian" side of the Gulf, the porosity of the tuff, became a social utopia and a structural ideal of philosophical texts.

In 1966, when Adorno took his third trip to Naples, he used the occasion to send postcard greetings to Sohn-Rethel with recollections of Capri and Positano—and to announce the publication of his latest major work, *Negative Dialectics.* Sohn-Rethel replied with a combination of enthusiasm and distress, taking issue with Adorno's diagnosis in the very first lines of the book that the attempt to change the world had gone awry. "That reads like the conclusion pertaining to a past that is over and done with. Are you so sure of that?"[2] Weren't the current events in China evidence that the social revolution still lay ahead? Eventually he appealed to Adorno's recollection of their conversation in Naples, which might indicate how much that conversation had circled around the possibility of revolution.

"The Benjamin conversation you're citing—my God, how the spirit of the age, or whatever you'd call it, has disregarded that,"[3] Adorno replied soberly. After World War II, after the experience of National Socialism and amid the perils of the Cold War, Naples in the 1920s seemed surreally distant to Adorno. But he was mistaken. Long before the advent of National Socialism, he had integrated the tellurian, "Homeric" side of the Gulf into his theory. The dialectical image originated in the hard limestone, the threat of water stopping up the holes, and the sea creatures in the aquarium in Naples. When National Socialism revealed the full extent of its demonic nature, Adorno's model of the dreadful demons from Positano proved an eerie fit.

Of all the participants in this meeting in Naples, Adorno was the most successful in his lifetime, a success that the others shared to various degrees. Benjamin did not survive fascism; he died in 1940 during his flight from the Nazis, in the town of Portbou at the French-Spanish border, but his writings were rediscovered in a stunning way in the 1970s, after Adorno had laid the groundwork, although Adorno's work on these writings was soon disparaged. Kracauer made a name for himself in America with his work on film, and did not go back to Germany. The friendship between Adorno and Kracauer remained intact until Kracauer's death, despite their ongoing squabbles. Adorno, trying to raise Kracauer's profile in Germany, successfully appealed to Siegfried Unseld, the publisher of Suhrkamp, to publish Kracauer's anthology *The Mass Ornament*. But Kracauer is still to be discovered for a broader audience as one of the most powerfully expressive feature writers of the 1920s and 30s. When Adorno and Sohn-Rethel resumed their correspondence in the late 1950s, their exchange was quite tentative, because Adorno did not want to go along with Sohn-Rethel's pushes for a revolution. Nevertheless, Sohn-Rethel struck up a conversation with Unseld at Adorno's funeral and enjoyed the belated satisfaction of having his works see publication and take hold in the 1970s, though their influence has largely fizzled out today.

Adorno's theory also appears to have missed out on an afterlife. Adorno fashioned the most consistent system out of the antisystematic idea of the constellation, thereby making it one of the most influential theories of European philosophy, which exhorted us not to forget the Shoah and functioned as a weapon against the denial of the abyss of modernity. The price for this systemization, however, was that the openness brought to bear by the constellation, its capacity for the integration of the marginal, was minimized.

But what *has* lived on is the stylistic activism of constellation, the materialism of form. It is one of the reasons for the lasting fascination with Adorno's texts. For us readers, these texts are magnificent by-products of this activism. Like musical scores, they are invitations to trace their constellations, to perform them anew, and consequently to practice offering resistance to any ideologizations.

Postlude

One of Adorno's most charming and playful texts is a little fantasia about a Capri fisherman, Spadaro, who became an icon of Capri tourism, his image photographed and reproduced on countless postcards. But Spadaro had not always been commodified into an image. "Before that he was just there—the simple man—and in the evenings, on the little boat, he helped illuminate the sea and its fish with his lantern, like a star, because it would have been too dark otherwise." But now that there were "a hundred seventy-five" pictures of him, "he himself has been symbolically lit up, through and through. He has made the sea and stars unnecessary, you might say."[1]

The same thing happened to Adorno. The many uses to which his texts have been applied have made him the figurehead of a philosophy that came to be known as Critical Theory, and this bright illumination harbors the risk that his texts could become invisible, "unnecessary, you might say."[2] But it is not always high season; Spadaro's symbolic illumination lets up, and the fishermen's own illumination is visible once more.

This book has aimed to accomplish the same for Adorno: to render visible the structural materiality of his texts. It has sought to portray the way a landscape can be transformed

Postcard (1933) of the fisherman Spadaro on Capri. Photo: akg-images.

into a momentous philosophical project. And it has sought to trace back the hypnotic circling in Adorno's texts, the dramatic journey into the underworld, and the blasting of hollow spaces. The source code for one of the most influential philosophical concepts of the twentieth century: comprising the eerie and stunningly beautiful landscape of the Gulf of Naples, the demons of the Amalfi Coast and the shimmering culture of Naples, the coolness of the locals and the phantasms of the visitors, the promise of a solidarity that emerges from a communal rhythm, and horrors from a deep, dark past that people have brought right back into the present.

Notes

INTRODUCTION

1. See Adorno, *Aspects of the New Right-Wing Extremism.*
2. Pabst, *Kindheit in Amorbach*; Steinert, *Adorno in Wien*; studies of Adorno in America include Ziege, *Antisemitismus und Gesellschafts-theorie,* and Jenemann, *Adorno in America.*
3. *Adorno: Eine Bildmonographie,* ed. Theodor W. Adorno Archiv, 206ff.
4. Von Haselberg, "Wiesengrund-Adorno," pp. 7–21, esp. p. 16.
5. Adorno and Berg, *Briefwechsel, 1925–1935,* p. 33.

CHAPTER 1. ISLAND OF HAPPINESS

1. La Capria, "Neapel als geistige Landschaft," p. 8.
2. Ibid.
3. Ibid.
4. Enzensberger, "Eine Theorie des Tourismus," pp. 190ff. All transla-tions are by Shelley Frisch, unless otherwise indicated.
5. Kracauer, "Die Wartenden," p. 383.
6. Wiggershaus, "Friedrich Pollock," pp. 751ff.
7. Horkheimer, "L'île heureuse," p. 302.
8. Savinio, *Capri,* pp. 6–7.
9. Sohn-Rethel, "Einige Unterbrechungen," p. 249.
10. Ibid., pp. 249ff.

11. Sohn-Rethel, "Aus einem Gespräch," p. 8.

12. Sohn-Rethel, "Exposee," p. 2.

13. Sohn-Rethel, "Aus einem Gespräch," p. 9.

14. Alfred Sohn-Rethel, *Erinnerungen.*

15. Adorno and Horkheimer, *Briefwechsel, 1927–1969,* 1: 278.

16. Benjamin, *Gesammelte Briefe,* 2: 467.

17. Benjamin, "Zwei Gedichte," p. 105.

18. Benjamin, *Gesammelte Briefe,* 2: 433.

19. Ibid.

20. Ibid., p. 474.

21. Savinio, *Capri,* p. 26.

22. Ibid.

23. Benjamin, *Gesammelte Briefe,* 2: 466.

24. Ibid., p. 473.

25. According to Sonnentag, *Spaziergänge,* p. 45. See also Cerio, *Capri,* pp. 155ff.

26. "On Capri there was a better Lenin, the splendid comrade, the jolly fellow with a lively and tireless interest in everything in the world, who treated people in an astonishingly mild manner." Quoted in Sonnentag, *Spaziergänge,* p. 37. See also Kesel, *Capri,* p. 272, and Cerio, *Capri,* p. 57. After the October Revolution, Capri also served as the point of entry for refugees fleeing the revolution. Cerio, *Capri,* p. 95. See also Money, *Capri,* p. 156.

27. Lacis, *Revolutionär im Beruf,* p. 42.

28. See, for example, Kaulen, "Walter Benjamin und Asja Lacis."

29. Benjamin, *Einbahnstraße,* p. 83; Benjamin, *Reflections,* p. 61.

30. Lacis, *Revolutionär im Beruf,* p. 43. For more on the meeting of Benjamin and Lacis, the minimizing of Lacis's significance for Benjamin, and the restitution of her significance in reception history, see Kaulen, "Walter Benjamin und Asja Lacis," and Buck-Morss, *Dialectics of Seeing,* pp. 30ff.

31. Benjamin, *Gesammelte Briefe,* 2: 451ff.

CHAPTER 2. TRAGIC HAUNTS

1. Adorno and Berg, *Briefwechsel, 1925–1935,* p. 24.

2. Ibid.

3. Subsequent quotations from *Adorno: Gesammelte Schriften* will be abbreviated as GS, followed by the volume and page numbers. This quotation can be found in GS 11: 388. Wherever the translator has quoted from English-language translations, these are cited in the notes, following the original German volume and page numbers. This quotation appears on p. 332 of Adorno's essay "The Curious Realist: On Siegfried Kracauer" in Adorno, *Notes to Literature,* pp. 332–47.

4. Kracauer, *Der Detektiv-Roman,* p. 117. This quotation appears on p. 173 of Kracauer's essay "The Hotel Lobby" on pp. 173–85 of Kraucauer, *The Mass Ornament.*

5. Löwenthal and Kracauer, *In steter Freundschaft,* pp. 46ff.

6. Adorno and Kracauer, "Der Riss der Welt," p. 138.

7. Morgenstern, *Alban Berg und seine Idole,* p. 120.

8. Adorno and Krenek, *Briefwechsel,* pp. 8ff.

9. Adorno and Kracauer, "Der Riss der Welt," p. 9.

10. Löwenthal and Kracauer, *In steter Freundschaft,* p. 32.

11. Ibid., p. 54.

12. Ibid., p. 32.

13. Ibid., p. 59.

14. Adorno and Berg, *Briefwechsel, 1925–1935,* pp. 24ff.

15. Adorno and Kracauer, "Der Riss der Welt," p. 176.

CHAPTER 3. A COMMON PURSUIT

1. GS 20: 173ff.

2. Sohn-Rethel, "Einige Unterbrechungen," p. 282.

3. Benjamin, *Gesammelte Briefe,* 2: 459.

4. Ibid., 2: 461.

5. Lukács, *Geschichte und Klassenbewusstsein,* pp. 176ff; Lukács, *History and Class Consciousness,* p. 88. For an analysis of the relation of Adorno's theories to Lukács, see Braunstein, *Adornos Kritik.*

6. Lukács, *Geschichte und Klassenbewusstsein,* p. 170; Lukács, *History and Class Consciousness,* p. 83.

7. Kracauer, "Die Reise und der Tanz," p. 219; Kracauer, "Travel and Dance," in *Mass Ornament,* pp. 65–73; p. 70.

8. Benjamin, *Gesammelte Briefe,* 2: 482ff. For information on the discussion about when Benjamin became acquainted with *History and Class Consciousness,* see Kaulen, "Walter Benjamin und Asja Lacis," p. 95.

9. Benjamin, *Ursprung des deutschen Trauerspiels,* p. 350; Benjamin, *Origin of German Tragic Drama,* p. 175.

10. Ibid.

11. Benjamin, *Ursprung des deutschen Trauerspiels,* p. 246; Benjamin, *Origin of German Tragic Drama,* p. 66.

12. Kracauer, *Der Detektiv-Roman,* p. 122.

13. Lukács, *Die Theorie des Romans,* p. 55; Lukács, *Theory of the Novel,* p. 64.

14. Preliminary draft of the "Imperial Panorama" section of *One-Way Street,* printed in: Benjamin, *Gesammelte Schriften,* 4: 933; Benjamin, *Reflections,* p. 74.

15. Sohn-Rethel, "Aus einem Gespräch," p. 5.

16. Sohn-Rethel, "Eine Verkehrsstockung," p. 9.

17. Ibid., p. 15.

CHAPTER 4. CHARNEL HOUSES

1. Sohn-Rethel, "Eine Verkehrsstockung," p. 13.

2. Ibid., p. 14.

3. Sohn-Rethel, "Das Ideal des Kaputten," p. 37.

4. Goethe, *Italienische Reise,* p. 245.

5. Sohn-Rethel, "Das Ideal des Kaputten," p. 38.

6. Ibid., p. 36.

7. Benjamin, *Ursprung des deutschen Trauerspiels,* p. 351; Benjamin, *Origin of German Tragic Drama,* p. 175.

8. Benjamin, *Ursprung des deutschen Trauerspiels,* p. 246; Benjamin, *Origin of German Tragic Drama,* p. 66. Osborne incorrectly translates "*einen* Mechanismus" as "*no* mechanism."

9. "Subjectivity, like an angel falling into the depths, is brought back by allegories, and is held fast in heaven, in God, by *ponderación misteriosa.*" Benjamin, *Ursprung des deutschen Trauerspiels,* p. 408; Benjamin, *Origin of German Tragic Drama,* p. 235.

10. Benjamin and Lacis, "Neapel," p. 311. For information on the "revival" of the category of porosity in more recent studies of the spatial structure and sociology of Naples, see Pisani, "Neapel-Topoi," esp. p. 37, where Pisani rightly claims that using porosity as a topos to describe Naples "dilutes its substance to the point of meaninglessness." Benjamin, *Reflections,* p. 168.

11. Benjamin and Lacis, "Neapel," p. 309; Benjamin, *Reflections,* p. 166.

12. Benjamin and Lacis, "Neapel," p. 316; Benjamin, *Reflections,* p. 172.

13. Bloch, "Italien und die Porosität," p. 509.

14. Mosebach, *Die schöne Gewohnheit,* p. 146.

15. Ibid., p. 138.

16. Ibid.

17. Benjamin and Lacis, "Neapel," p. 309; Benjamin, *Reflections,* p. 165.

18. Ibid.

19. Ibid. For information on the modern legacy of porous construction, see Maak, *Der Architekt am Strand,* pp. 194ff.

20. Hildegard Brenner opened her afterword to *Revolutionär im Beruf* with this remark: "The name Asja Lacis ought to have been included a full two decades ago by those who knew the historical connections. This did not happen. When the edition of Benjamin's *Schriften* was published in 1955, the dedication of *One-Way Street* to his 'Girlfriend in Riga' had been removed, and the name Lacis as co-author of the essay 'Naples' deleted" (Lacis, *Revolutionär im Beruf,* p. 121). Kaulen describes the conflict in "Walter Benjamin und Asja

Lacis." For Adorno's response to the basic charge that this was a tendentious publication, see GS 20: 182–86.

21. See also Mosebach, *Die schöne Gewohnheit,* pp. 53ff.

22. Benjamin and Lacis, "Neapel," p. 310; Benjamin, *Reflections,* p. 167.

23. Lacis, *Revolutionär im Beruf,* p. 33.

24. Benjamin, "Zwei Gedichte," p. 112.

25. Ibid. This linking technique may have been a holdover from Benjamin's study of early German Romanticism in the course of writing his dissertation. For information on linking in early German Romanticism, see Menninghaus, *Unendliche Verdopplung,* pp. 179ff.

26. Detlev Schöttker has pointed out an additional source of influence for Benjamin, which he may have put to new use in the Neapolitan constellation: "Benjamin came in contact with constructivism by 1924 at the latest, when he translated a brief article by Tristan Tzara about the photographer Man Ray for the constructivist journal *G.*" Schöttker, *Konstruktiver Fragmentarismus,* p. 158.

27. Benjamin, *Gesammelte Briefe,* 2: 480.

28. "He can't break the habit of stealing," Benjamin once wrote in a letter. Benjamin, *Gesammelte Briefe,* 2: 511.

29. Even the contrast between the Italian manner of entering a restaurant and the German way of laying claim to tables is found in the preliminary draft of the essay on Naples, directly preceding the programmatic "The stamp of the definitive is avoided." Preliminary draft of Benjamin and Lacis, "Neapel," The National Library of Israel, ARC.4° 1598/96, p. 4.

30. Bloch, "Italien und die Porosität," p. 515.

31. Ibid., p. 513.

32. Ibid., p. 514.

33. Ibid., p. 508.

34. Susan Buck-Morss regards this as a stylistic experiment: "There is no lack of humor or entertainment. There is no explicit political message. Rather, hardly noticeable to the reader, an experiment is underway, how images, gathered by a person walking the streets of a city, can be interpreted against the grain of idealist literary style. The images are not subjective impressions, but objective expressions." Buck-Morss, *Dialectics of Seeing,* p. 27.

35. Preliminary draft of Benjamin and Lacis, "Neapel," The National Library of Israel, ARC.4° 1598/96. Klaus Garber has pointed this out in his book *Zum Bilde Walter Benjamins,* p. 175: "Benjamin structured his text in only five sections (each marked by a space in the critical edition); the fragmentation of the text into innumerable additional sections was an editorial addition for the purpose of printing it in the newspaper."

36. McGill holds Benjamin's theatrical turn responsible for his change of style: "He turned from taking drama primarily as a literary object of study and interpretation to enacting a kind of improvised theatre in the construction of his own texts. From *One-Way-Street* to the enormous, unfinished work of the *Arcades Project,* Benjamin began to create texts that did not present a philosophical argument in a linear manner, but rather set out a series of aphoristic or meticulously observed passages, like so many thematically connected scenes in an improvised piece of theatre that has no overarching plot, no single directorial vision guiding the performance." McGill, "Porous Coupling," p. 64. For McGill, the porous became a metaphor for the displacement of gender stereotypes when Benjamin worked with Lacis (ibid., p. 70).

37. Graeme Gilloch points this out in his comment that the literary form "mimics the rhythm and tempo of metropolitan life." Gilloch, *Myth and Metropolis,* p. 24. Benjamin takes this mimesis a step further after his essay on Naples, stating that the book *One-Way Street* is itself constructed like a street: "My 'aphorisms' has become a remarkable organization or construction, a street." Benjamin, *Gesammelte Briefe,* 3: 197. See also Schöttker, *Konstruktiver Fragmentarismus,* pp. 181ff.

38. Bredekamp, *Darwins Korallen.*

39. For more on this subject, see Deleuze and Guattari, "Introduction."

CHAPTER 5. MUSIC FROM VOLCANIC ROCK

1. Benjamin and Lacis, "Neapel," p. 316; Benjamin, *Reflections,* 172–73.

2. Adorno, "So müßte ich ein Engel," p. 97.

3. Adorno and Kracauer, "Der Riss der Welt," p. 111.

4. Adorno and Berg, *Briefwechsel, 1925–1935,* p. 59.

5. Ibid., p. 39.

6. Ibid.; italics in the original text.

7. Ibid., p. 43.

8. Ibid., p. 44.

9. GS 13: 393.

10. GS 13: 33.

11. GS 13: 43.

12. GS 11: 471.

13. GS 11: 28, 31, 32.

14. GS 7: 541.

CHAPTER 6. STAR FORMATIONS

1. Benjamin's next essay that centered on a city—Moscow—brought the concept of porosity to bear only in the follow-up terms *prisma, permeation,* and *constellation* (Benjamin, "Moskau," esp. pp. 319, 330, 335). In the *Arcades Project* the word *porosity* appears solely in a peripheral note, stripped of its utopian connection (Benjamin, *Das Passagen-Werk,* p. 292).

2. Lukács, *Die Theorie des Romans,* p. 21; Lukács, *Theory of the Novel,* p. 29.

3. Benjamin, *Goethes Wahlverwandtschaften,* pp. 200ff.

4. Benjamin, *Ursprung des deutschen Trauerspiels,* p. 214; Benjamin, *Origin of German Tragic Drama,* p. 34.

5. Benjamin, *Ursprung des deutschen Trauerspiels,* p. 934.

6. See Kleinwort, "Zur Desorientierung," esp. p. 104.

7. Benjamin, *Ursprung des deutschen Trauerspiels,* p. 215; Benjamin, *Origin of German Tragic Drama,* p. 34.

8. Benjamin, *Ursprung des deutschen Trauerspiels,* p. 879. See also Buck-Morss, *Dialectics of Seeing,* pp. 15–20.

9. Norbert Bolz and Richard Faber discuss this markedly new direction occasioned by "his stay in Capri in 1924 and his encounter with Asja Lacis," in their book *Antike und Moderne,* p. 16.

10. "It is not just the final 'stage,' but rather the 'constellation' of all of them that 'portrays' the 'idea' of the tragic drama allegory without 'having' it in a concluding sentence." Menninghaus, *Walter Benjamins Theorie,* p. 97.

11. GS 11: 571; Adorno, *Notes to Literature,* p. 223.

12. GS 1: 335. This statement echoes Marx's *Capital,* in which the mysteries of the commodity form disappear as soon as their structure is revealed. Karl Marx, *Das Kapital,* p. 63.

13. Adorno himself suggested as much, as in this comment: "Dialectical images are constellations between alienated things and inchoate meaning, pausing at a moment of indifference between death and meaning." Adorno and Benjamin, *Briefwechsel, 1928–1940,* p. 152. Benjamin had already linked the constellation and the dialectical image; Friedlander, for example, integrates the constellation from the "Epistemo-Critical Prologue" into his interpretation of Benjamin's dialectical image as a matter of course. Friedlander, "Measure of the Contingent," esp. pp. 10ff.

14. Russian formalism may have been the connecting link in Asja Lacis's mediation. On this issue, see Jurij Striedter's remarks about the fact that Benjamin's essay "The Storyteller" invoked the same author—Nikolai Leskov—as had one of the major protagonists of Russian formalism, Boris Eikhenbaum. See Striedter, "Zur formalistischen Theorie," esp. p. lvii.

CHAPTER 7. POSTCARDS

1. Richter, "Das blaue Feuer der Romantik," p. 78.

2. Fontane, *Werke,* 2: 488.

3. Benjamin, *Gesammelte Schriften,* 6; 694. See also Walter Benjamin Archiv, ed., *Bilder, Texte und Zeichen,* p. 138. The letter is published in Benjamin, *Gesammelte Briefe,* 3: 177.

4. GS 17: 23.

5. Postcard dated March 22, 1925, Deutsches Literaturarchiv Marbach, letters to Ernst Georg and Lily Jünger, access number: HS.2005.0060.

6. GS 17: 80.

7. GS 17: 26.

8. GS 17: 25.

9. GS 17: 23.

CHAPTER 8. SKELETONS AND SPECTERS

1. Savinio, *Capri*, p. 44.

2. La Capria, "Neapel als geistige Landschaft," p. 9.

3. Ibid.

4. Quoted in Gruner, "Ein Schicksal," p. 112.

5. Quoted in Reich, *Im Wettlauf*, p. 275.

6. Benjamin, review of Job, *Neapel*, p. 133.

7. Kracauer, review of von Hatzfeld, *Positano*, p. 6.

8. Quoted in ibid.

9. Adorno and Kracauer, "Der Riss der Welt," p. 174.

10. Ibid., p. 176.

11. Kracauer, "Felsenwahn in Positano," p. 297.

12. Ibid.

13. Ibid., p. 298.

14. Marx, *Das Kapital*, p. 90; Marx, *Capital*, p. 169.

15. Marx, *Das Kapital*, p. 87; Marx, *Capital*, p. 165.

16. Marx, *Das Kapital*, p. 86; Marx, *Capital*, p. 165.

17. Marx, *Das Kapital*, p. 91; Marx, *Capital*, p. 170.

18. Sohn-Rethel, *Erinnerungen*.

19. According to the Baedeker guide, "registration at the gatekeeper on the second floor with a visiting card; tip." Baedeker, *Italien von den Alpen bis Neapel*, p. 378.

20. Many thanks to Christiane Groeben, the archivist at the Zoological Station, for this discovery.

21. Kracauer, "Felsenwahn in Positano," p. 303.

22. *Leitfaden für das Aquarium der Zoologischen Station zu Neapel*, p. 85.

23. Klee, *Briefe an die Familie*, 1: 220. He wrote in his diary, "a congealed, angelic little animal <transparent—spiritual>." Klee, *Tagebücher*,

p. 123. Klee's adjective for the congealed creature (*gallertartig*) recalls Marx's use of the term *Gallerte* in *Capital*.

24. Marx, *Das Kapital,* p. 52; Marx, *Capital,* p. 128. Blumenberg provides the reference for the connection between water and money in the term liquidity. Blumenberg, *Schiffbruch mit Zuschauer,* p. 11. Marx uses the term *Arbeitsgallerte* for this congealed quantity.

25. Sohn-Rethel, "Exposee," p. 72.

26. Ibid., p. 73.

27. Hagen, "Davor hatte ich eine instinktive Abzirkelung," p. 4.

28. *Neapel und Umgebung,* p. 19. This travel guide is part of the literary estate containing Kracauer's library that is housed at the Deutsches Literaturarchiv in Marbach; it is classified as "Krac: 5." Two admission tickets to the temple in Paestum—stamped September 24, 1925—that were found in the book indicate that this was the travel guide that Kracauer and Adorno had with them. The Baedeker travel guide states that the exhibition was located "across from the collection (Mostra) of dissected marine animals." Baedeker, *Italien von den Alpen bis Neapel,* p. 378.

29. Heuss, *Anton Dohrn in Neapel,* p. 156. For more on Lo Bianco, see the fine portrait in Douglas, *Looking Back,* pp. 180–82.

30. Georg Büchner, the writer and natural scientist, also encountered this problem in 1836 in Strasbourg when he examined the nervous system of the common barbel; because alcohol was used in the preparation process, significant differences in color were lost.

31. "Sur des pièces conservées dans l'alcool il est impossible de distinguer ces filets." Georg Büchner, "Mémoire sur le système nerveux du Barbeau," p. 27. See also Roth, *Georg Büchners,* p. 75.

32. Heuss, *Anton Dohrn in Neapel,* p. 156. It would therefore appear that Adorno was not seeing Lo Bianco's specimens for the first time while in Naples. A report issued in 1873 by the Senckenberg Society for Nature Research in Frankfurt states, "Herr Prof. Dr. A. Dohrn, son of the famous entomologist, has implemented an idea that is extremely meritorious for scientific endeavors, namely to establish an aquarium in Naples, at the shore of the rich and splendid Mediterranean, as an international physiological observation and research station.

Toward this end, which will be so very useful for science, Herr Marcus Goldschmidt has loaned capital in the amount of 1000 thalers, requesting that the accrued interest is reimbursed annually in the form of payment in kind, to be used by the Senckenberg Society for Nature Research. The first of these interest payments arrived here today." Von Fritsch, *Bericht über die Senckenbergische,* p. 11. This would not be the last payment of this sort. During Adorno's visits to the Senckenberg Museum as a schoolchild (Pabst, *Kindheit in Amorbach,* p. 94), the preserving jars were likely seen as juicy objects of horror.

CHAPTER 9. THE ART AND SCIENCE OF INSERTION

1. Bloch, "Italien und die Porosität," pp. 513ff. See also Dieter Richter: "Walter Benjamin's and Ernst Bloch's famous category of 'porosity' is nothing other than the draft of an urbanistic and intellectual counterproject to modernity's manifestations of alienation." Richter, *Neapel,* p. 235.

2. GS 1: 364. Adorno, "Idea of Natural History," pp. 123–24.

3. D'Iorio, *Le voyage de Nietzsche.*

4. Colli and Montinari, eds., *Briefe an Friedrich Nietzsche,* 1: 320.

5. Nietzsche, *Digitale Kritische Gesamtausgabe,* § 3 eKGWB/EH-MA-3.

6. Ibid., § 6 eKGWB/EH-MA-3.

7. Theodor W. Adorno Archiv, ed., "Adornos Seminar," p. 56.

8. *Neapel und Umgebung,* p. 76.

9. Baedeker, *Italien von den Alpen bis Neapel,* p. 426. See also Fiorentino, *Memorie di Sorrento,* pp. 177ff.

10. Benjamin, *Ursprung des deutschen Trauerspiels,* p. 359; Benjamin, *Origin of German Tragic Drama,* p. 183.

11. Lo Bianco, "Metodi usati."

12. Schiemenz, review of Lo Bianco's *Metodi usati,* p. 54.

13. *Leitfaden für das Aquarium der Zoologischen Station zu Neapel,* p. 54.

14. Benjamin, *Ursprung des deutschen Trauerspiels,* p. 359; Benjamin, *Origin of German Tragic Drama,* p. 184. Osborne's misleading "He places it within it, and stands behind it" has been changed to: "He inserts it within, and reaches down there."

15. Benjamin, "Möbel und Masken," p. 478.

16. Ibid.

17. Ibid., p. 477.

18. GS 17: 21.

19. Benjamin, *Ursprung des deutschen Trauerspiels,* p. 388; Benjamin, *Origin of German Tragic Drama,* p. 215.

20. GS 2: 77; Adorno, *Kierkegaard,* p. 52.

21. Adorno and Benjamin, *Briefwechsel, 1928–1940,* p. 152.

22. GS 2: 119; Adorno, *Kierkegaard,* p. 83.

23. Habermas, *Der philosophische Diskurs,* p. 144; Habermas, "Entwinement of Myth and Enlightenment," p. 119.

24. Kracauer, "Der verbotene Blick," p. 226.

25. Ibid., p. 227.

26. GS 17: 15ff.; Adorno, *Beethoven: The Philosophy of Music,* p. 125.

CHAPTER 10. BLASTING OUT LIVING SPACE

1. Szeemann, "Gilbert Clavel," p. 249.

2. Thomas Schmitt and Thomas Steinfeld structured their documentary on Capri, *Exil, Eden, Endstation,* around these construction projects.

3. Sonnentag, *Spaziergänge,* p. 64.

4. Kantorowicz, *Meine Kleider,* p. 37.

5. Staatsarchiv Basel, PA 969, letter to the editors of *Annalen,* dated September 30, 1927.

6. Kracauer, "Felsenwahn in Positano," p. 299.

7. Staatsarchiv Basel, PA 969, letter to the editors of *Annalen,* dated September 30, 1927.

8. Ibid.

9. *Berliner Illustrirte Zeitung* 33, no. 45 (November 9, 1924): 1344. In 1938 the *Hamburger Illustrierte* would accompany a lavishly illustrated two-page spread with the question, "Would you like to live this way, too?" *Hamburger Illustrierte* 20, no. 41 (October 1, 1938): 6ff.

10. Cerio, *Mein Capri,* p. 29. René Clavel wrote, "The material there, a kind of limestone, is extremely hard, and thorough blasting is the

only way of working with it." Staatsarchiv Basel, PA 969, letter to the editors of *Annalen,* dated September 30, 1927.

11. Grotzinger and Jordan, *Understanding Earth,* p. 131.

12. Nachlass, Staatsarchiv Basel, PA 969, letter dated March 29, 1926.

13. Szeemann, "Gilbert Clavel," p. 284. Clavel also gives metaphysical pride of place to these hollows: "I want to dig, dig deep, but not to make burrows, the way a mole would. I want to create wide open pits (shafts) that everyone can peer down into. When light falls into the depths, the gold gleams. Without light it's all dead." Diary entry dated November 12, 1911, Nachlass, Staatsarchiv Basel, PA 969.

14. Clavel, *Mein Bereich,* p. 39.

15. Szeemann, "Gilbert Clavel," p. 278.

16. Kracauer, "Felsenwahn in Positano," p. 299.

17. Ibid.

18. Clavel, *Mein Bereich,* p. 23.

CHAPTER 11. TOURING THE CRATER

1. For the tavern scene he used the terms "caesura in the Hölderlinian sense" and "expressionless" (Adorno and Berg, *Briefwechsel, 1925–1935,* p. 51), terms from Benjamin's essay on Goethe's *Elective Affinities,* which he had previously criticized so roundly.

2. Ibid., pp. 74ff.

3. GS 18: 462.

4. Adorno and Berg, *Briefwechsel, 1925–1935,* p. 58.

5. Benjamin and Lacis, "Neapel," p. 309; Benjamin, *Reflections,* p. 166.

6. Adorno and Berg, *Briefwechsel, 1925–1935,* p. 75.

7. Ibid., pp. 87ff.

8. GS 18: 461.

9. GS 18: 474.

10. Kant, *Kritik der Urteilskraft,* p. 107.

11. Ibid.

12. Ibid., p. 106.

13. Groys, "Die Stadt im Zeitalter," p. 191.

14. "And by means of Thos. Cook & Son's electric railway the visit is now rendered easy and agreeable, and not too tiring for even delicate persons," the 1924 Cook's travel guide tells readers. *Cook's Handbook,* p. 84.

15. Smith, "Thomas Cook," esp. p. 14.

16. Richter, *Neapel,* p. 189.

17. Szeemann, "Gilbert Clavel," p. 287.

18. Sohn-Rethel, "Vesuvbesteigung 1926," p. 28.

19. Baedeker, *Unteritalien,* p. 136.

20. Sohn-Rethel, "Vesuvbesteigung 1926," p. 30.

21. Kracauer, "Felsenwahn in Positano," p. 296.

22. Hegel, *Enzyklopädie der philosophischen,* 8: 60.

23. GS 17: 21.

24. Unfortunately, the second section is not set off as such in the print layout in the *Gesammelte Schriften,* nor can it be seen in the 1964 edition of the *Moments musicaux,* because the typesetting forgoes indentations in both editions and the previous line ends flush right. This section should begin after the words "but crystalline" (17, 23), as we see in the printed image of the initial publication in: *Die Musik* 1 (1928): 4. See Adorno, *Moments musicaux,* p. 23.

25. GS 17: 25.

26. For this and the following quotations: GS 17: 27 and 28.

CHAPTER 12. SNAKELIKE ENTRAILS

1. Benjamin, *Gesammelte Briefe,* 2: 480.

2. Sohn-Rethel, *Das Ideal des Kaputten,* p. 33.

3. "Gloomy box of the Nordic house": Benjamin and Lacis, "Neapel," p. 310, Benjamin, *Reflections,* p. 167; "flood out": Benjamin and Lacis, "Neapel," p. 314, Benjamin, *Reflections,* p. 171; "street and home": Benjamin and Lacis, "Neapel," p. 315, Benjamin, *Reflections,* p. 172; "public sphere": Bloch, "Italien und die Porosität," p. 510.

4. Benjamin, *Einbahnstrasse,* p. 89; Benjamin, *Reflections,* pp. 64–65.

5. Kracauer, "Felsenwahn in Positano," p. 300.

6. Ibid., pp. 299ff.

7. Douglas, *Looking Back,* p. 35.

8. Obituary by Emil Henk, typescript, p. 2. Staatsarchiv Basel, Nachlass Gilbert Clavel.

9. "Since we have just been talking about procreation and birth, I would like to take this opportunity to remind you of my old testicle, which is being stored in a preserving jar in Kleinhüningen. I told Mama she should pour some liquid (formaldehyde or some other preservative) on the lost egg to keep it from constantly drying out. Later on, when the price of gold goes back down, I'll have Sauter make me a golden capsule for it so I can carry my egg in my pocket as a talisman. When the time is right, I will also place it in the hand of a beautiful woman, and let her take a guess!!" Szeemann, "Gilbert Clavel," p. 100.

10. Ibid., pp. 280ff.

11. Kracauer, "Felsenwahn in Positano," p. 300.

12. Szeemann, "Gilbert Clavel," p. 288.

13. Kracauer, "Felsenwahn in Positano," p. 300.

14. *Berliner Illustrirte Zeitung* 33, no. 45 (November 9, 1924): 1344.

15. Quoted in Gumnior and Ringguth, *Horkheimer,* p. 16.

16. Wiggershaus, "Friedrich Pollock," p. 750.

17. Ibid., p. 754.

18. For example, with Philipp Lenhard's edition of Pollock's collected works since 2018 and Lenhard's biography *Friedrich Pollock.*

19. Gangl, "Staatskapitalismus und Dialektik," esp. p. 159.

20. Wiggershaus, "Friedrich Pollock," p. 755.

21. Adorno and Horkheimer, *Briefwechsel, 1927–1969,* 2: 139ff.

22. This discussion is embedded in a broader dispute about the correct (or more sharply defined) term for the new economic system. For details, see Wiggershaus, *Die Frankfurter Schule,* pp. 314ff. Wiggershaus remarks that the ongoing debate (primarily between Pollock and Franz Neumann, the author of *Behemoth*) about the right de-

scriptive term—state capitalism or monopoly capitalim—in analyzing this economic system was a mere "quarrel about words" (ibid., p. 324).

23. Gangl, "Staatskapitalismus und Dialektik," p. 159.

24. GS 4: 64.

25. Sohn-Rethel, *Erinnerungen.*

26. Kant, *Metaphysics of Morals,* p. 277.

27. Markus Fahlbusch wrote: "The reception history of the essay 'On Jazz' makes it clear that it is one of Adorno's most difficult and problematic texts. The essay was both vehemently criticized and politely ignored, but seldom taken seriously as a substantive contribution to an actual theory of jazz." Fahlbusch, "Über Jazz," p. 20. See also Steinert, *Die Entdeckung der Kulturindustrie.*

CHAPTER 13. THE TREASURELESS
TROVE OF THE FUNCTIONING

1. Quoted in Richter, "Das blaue Feuer der Romantik," p. 88.

2. Ibid., p. 80.

3. Machatschek, *Golf von Neapel,* pp. 246ff.

4. Steinfeld, *Der Arzt von San Michele,* pp. 176ff.

5. Kempter, "Nachwort," esp. p. 99. Richter, "Friedrich Alfred Krupp auf Capri," p. 175. See also Norman Douglas's furious defense in his memoir, *Looking Back,* pp. 182ff.

6. Gregorovius, *Wanderjahre in Italien,* 3: 23.

7. Andersen, *Aus Andersens Tagebüchern,* p. 189. Quoted in Gay, *Bourgeois Experience,* 1: 112.

8. This translation, by Geoffrey Wall, appears on p. 227 of "Gustave Flaubert: Eleven Letters"; it is from a letter from Flaubert to Camille Rogier, dated March 11, 1851.

9. Munthe, *Story of San Michele,* p. 126.

10. Preliminary draft of Benjamin and Lacis, "Neapel," The National Library of Israel, ARC.4° 1598/96, p. 1.

11. Benjamin and Lacis, "Neapel," p. 316; Benjamin, *Reflections,* p. 173.

12. GS 17: 95; Adorno, "On Jazz," p. 488.

13. GS 17: 76; Adorno, "On Jazz," p. 471.

14. GS 17: 86; Adorno, "On Jazz," p. 480.

15. GS 17: 78; Adorno, "On Jazz," p. 473.

16. GS 17: 79; Adorno, "On Jazz," p. 475.

17. GS 17: 80ff.; Adorno, "On Jazz," p. 476.

18. GS 17: 81; Adorno, "On Jazz," p. 476.

19. "It is not old and repressed instincts which are freed in the form of standardized rhythms and standardized explosive outbursts; it is new, repressed, and mutilated instincts which have stiffened into the masks of those in the distant past." GS 17: 84; Adorno, "On Jazz," p. 478.

20. GS 17: 84; Adorno, "On Jazz," p. 478.

21. GS 17: 86; Adorno, "On Jazz," p. 480.

22. GS 17: 87; Adorno, "On Jazz," p. 481.

23. GS 17: 89; Adorno, "On Jazz," p. 483.

24. GS 17: 89; Adorno, "On Jazz," pp. 482–83. A small example in this section clearly reveals the contrast between Adorno's earlier and current specification of the constellation model. In his book about Kierkegaard, typographical errors were still ciphers that emancipated themselves from the subjective need for expression, and were thus a component of the constellation of the aesthetic. In the essay on jazz they contributed to the vibrato, serving to loosen up rigidity by means of apparent dilettantism.

25. GS 17: 91; Adorno, "On Jazz," p. 484.

26. "If one wanted to describe the phenomenon of interference in jazz in terms of broad and solid concepts of style, one could claim it as the combination of salon music and march music. The former represents an individuality which in truth is none at all, but merely the socially produced illusion of it; the latter is an equally fictive community which is formed from nothing other than the alignment of atoms under the force that is exerted upon them" (GS 17: 91ff.; Adorno, "On Jazz," p. 485).

27. GS 17: 92; Adorno, "On Jazz," p. 486.

28. GS 17: 93; Adorno, "On Jazz," p. 486.

29. GS 17: 95; Adorno, "On Jazz," p. 488.

30. GS 17: 93; Adorno, "On Jazz," p. 486.

31. GS 17: 96; Adorno, "On Jazz," p. 488.

32. Sohn-Rethel, "Das Ideal des Kaputten," p. 36.

33. Ibid., p. 38.

34. GS 4: 52; Adorno, *Minima Moralia,* p. 47.

35. Adorno and Horkheimer, *Briefwechsel, 1927–1969,* 1: 173.

36. Ibid., 1: 160.

37. Adorno and Horkheimer, *Briefwechsel, 1927–1969,* 1: 170.

38. Ibid., 1: 169.

39. Ibid., 1: 173.

40. GS 17: 100; Adorno, "On Jazz," p. 491.

41. Ibid.

CHAPTER 14. PARTHENOPE WASHES ASHORE

1. Szeemann, "Gilbert Clavel," p. 256.

2. Ibid., p. 260.

3. Norton, *Leonide Massine,* p. 278.

4. Spina, "Der Mythos der Sirene Parthenope," pp. 23–27.

5. Then she was served on a silver platter to the generals at a ceremonial dinner as "siren in mayonnaise," in Curzio Malaparte's novel *The Skin,* pp. 225 and 227.

6. Adorno, *Briefe an die Eltern, 1939–1951,* p. 294.

7. Ibid.

8. The swimming "antiquity" that once served Odysseus on his journeys; the bed that can't be moved. Kracauer, "Felsenwahn in Positano," p. 297.

9. GS 3: 31; Adorno and Horkheimer, *Dialectic of Enlightenment,* p. 10.

10. GS 3: 31; Adorno and Horkheimer, *Dialectic of Enlightenment,* pp. 10–11.

11. GS 7: 489ff.; Adorno, *Aesthetic Theory,* p. 331.

12. In the typescript, the individual sections are set off even more clearly with asterisks. Theodor W. Adorno Archiv, Frankfurt am Main, Ts 0498, pp. 18 and 33.

13. GS 3: 58; Adorno and Horkheimer, *Dialectic of Enlightenment,* p. 32.

14. GS 3: 60; Adorno and Horkheimer, *Dialectic of Enlightenment,* p. 34.

CHAPTER 15. BLOOD MIRACLE IN LITTLE ITALY

1. The exact dates of the trip are difficult to reconstruct. On September 12, 1925, Adorno wrote to Berg from Capri; he spent September 24 in Paestum. Since, according to his own statement, he was in Naples at the beginning of his trip and shortly before he departed, it is quite unlikely that he was in Naples on September 19.

2. GS 3: 203; Adorno and Horkheimer, *Dialectic of Enlightenment,* p. 147.

3. GS 3: 95; Adorno, *Dialectic of Enlightenment,* p. 59.

4. The stream of blood in the epigraph for the Schubert essay is one of the few exceptions. See also Winfried Menninghaus, who comments, in reference to Benjamin's destruction without bloodshed, "that Benjamin's systematic devaluation of blood seems directed against any kind of biologistic racism." Menninghaus, "Das Ausdruckslose," p. 67.

5. GS 3: 91; Adorno and Horkheimer, *Dialectic of Enlightenment,* p. 56.

6. Adorno, *Briefe an die Eltern, 1939–1951,* p. 190.

7. GS 3: 94; Adorno and Horkheimer, *Dialectic of Enlightenment,* p. 59.

8. GS 11: 39; Adorno, "On Epic Naiveté," in *Notes to Literature,* pp. 48–52; this passage appears on p. 52.

9. GS 2: 65. Adorno, *Kierkegaard: Construction of the Aesthetic,* p. 43.

10. GS 11: 34; Adorno, "On Epic Naiveté," p. 48.

11. Ibid.

12. Ibid.

13. For the history of this metaphor, see Blumenberg, *Schiffbruch mit Zuschauer,* p. 56.

14. See Platthaus, *Höllenfahrten,* pp. 95ff.

15. GS 3: 95; Adorno and Horkheimer, *Dialectic of Enlightenment,* p. 59.

16. Ibid.

CHAPTER 16. THE PROPHECY OF POSITANO

1. "The Scribble-In-Book I," Theodor W. Adorno Archiv, Frankfurt am Main, ms. 19.

2. GS 10: 257; Adorno, "Notes on Kafka," pp. 246–47.

3. GS 10: 267. Adorno, "Notes on Kafka," p. 254.

4. GS 10: 268. Adorno, "Notes on Kafka," p. 256.

5. GS 10: 273. Adorno, "Notes on Kafka," p. 259.

6. GS 17: 18.

CHAPTER 17. AFTERLIFE

1. Gumbrecht, *In 1926.*

2. Adorno and Sohn-Rethel, *Briefwechsel, 1936–1969,* pp. 150ff.

3. Ibid., pp. 152ff.

POSTLUDE

1. GS 20: 583–84.

2. Ibid.

Bibliography

Adorno: Eine Bildmonographie. Ed. Theodor W. Adorno Archiv. Frankfurt am Main: Suhrkamp, 2003.

Adorno, Theodor W. *Aesthetic Theory.* Trans. Robert Hullot-Kentor. Minneapolis: University of Minnesota Press, 1997.

———. *Aspects of the New Right-Wing Extremism.* Trans. Wieland Hoban. Malden, MA: Polity, 2020.

———. *Beethoven: Philosophie der Musik.* Ed. Rolf Tiedemann. Frankfurt am Main: Suhrkamp, 2004.

———. *Beethoven: The Philosophy of Music.* Ed. Rolf Tiedemann. Trans. Edmund Jephcott. Malden, MA: Polity Press, 1998.

———. *Briefe an die Eltern, 1939–1951.* Ed. Christoph Gödde and Henri Lonitz. Frankfurt am Main: Suhrkamp, 2003.

———. *Gesammelte Schriften.* Ed. Rolf Tiedemann et al. Frankfurt am Main: Suhrkamp, 1970–86.

———. "The Idea of Natural History." Trans. Robert Hullot-Kentor. *Telos,* no. 60 (Summer 1984): 111–24.

———. *Kierkegaard: Construction of the Aesthetic.* Trans. Robert Hullot-Kentor. Minneapolis: University of Minnesota Press, 1989.

———. *Minima Moralia.* Trans. Edmund Jephcott. New York: Verso, 1974.

———. *Moments musicaux.* Frankfurt am Main: Suhrkamp, 1964.

———. "Notes on Kafka." In *Prisms,* trans. Shierry Weber Nicholsen and Samuel Weber, pp. 243–70. Cambridge, MA: MIT Press, 1983.

———. *Notes to Literature.* Ed. Rolf Tiedemann. Trans. Shierry Weber Nicolsen. New York: Columbia University Press, 2019.

————. "Schubert." *Die Musik* 1 (1928): 1–12.

————. *So müßte ich ein Engel und kein Autor sein: Der Briefwechsel mit Peter Suhrkamp und Siegfried Unseld*. Ed. Wolfgang Schopf. Frankfurt am Main: Suhrkamp, 2003.

————. *Zu einer Theorie der musikalischen Reproduktion*. Ed. Henri Lonitz. Frankfurt am Main: Suhrkamp, 2005.

Adorno, Theodor W., and Walter Benjamin. *Briefwechsel, 1928–1940*. Ed. Henri Lonitz. Frankfurt am Main: Suhrkamp, 1995.

Adorno, Theodor W., and Alban Berg. *Briefwechsel, 1925–1935*. Ed. Henri Lonitz. Frankfurt am Main: Suhrkamp, 1997.

Adorno, Theodor W., and Max Horkheimer. *Briefwechsel, 1927–1969*. 4 vols. Ed. Christoph Gödde and Henri Lonitz. Frankfurt am Main: Suhrkamp, 2003–6.

Adorno, Theodor W., and Siegfried Kracauer. *Der Riss der Welt geht auch durch mich: Briefwechsel, 1923–1966*. Ed. Wolfgang Schopf. Frankfurt am Main: Suhrkamp, 2008.

Adorno, Theodor W., and Ernst Krenek. *Briefwechsel*. Ed. Wolfgang Rogge. Frankfurt am Main: Suhrkamp, 1974.

Adorno, Theodor W., and Thomas Mann. *Briefwechsel, 1943–1955*. Ed. Christoph Gödde and Thomas Sprecher. Frankfurt am Main: Suhrkamp, 2002.

Adorno, Theodor W., and Alfred Sohn-Rethel. *Briefwechsel, 1936–1969*. Ed. Christoph Gödde. Munich: Edition Text + Kritik, 1991.

Baedeker, Karl. *Italien von den Alpen bis Neapel: Handbuch für Reisende*. Leipzig: Baedeker, 1926.

————. *Unteritalien: Sizilien Malta Tripolis Korfu; Handbuch für Reisende*. Leipzig: Baedeker, 1936.

Barthes, Roland. "The Structuralist Activity." In Roland Barthes, *Critical Essays*, trans. Richard Howard, pp. 213–20. Evanston, IL: Northwestern University Press, 1972.

Benjamin, Walter. *Das Kunstwerk im Zeitalter seiner technischen Reproduzierbarkeit*. In *Gesammelte Schriften*, 7 vols., ed. Rolf Tiedemann and Hermann Schweppenhäuser, 7: 350–84. Frankfurt am Main: Suhrkamp, 1972–99.

————. *Das Passagen-Werk.* In *Gesammelte Schriften,* 7 vols., ed. Rolf Tiedemann and Hermann Schweppenhäuser, vol. 5. Frankfurt am Main: Suhrkamp, 1972–99.

————. "Der Autor als Produzent." In *Gesammelte Schriften,* 7 vols., ed. Rolf Tiedemann and Hermann Schweppenhäuser, 2: 683–701. Frankfurt am Main: Suhrkamp, 1972–99.

————. "Disputation bei Meyerhold." In *Gesammelte Schriften,* 7 vols., ed. Rolf Tiedemann and Hermann Schweppenhäuser, 4: 481–83. Frankfurt am Main: Suhrkamp, 1972–99.

————. "Ein Aussenseiter macht sich bemerkbar." In *Gesammelte Schriften,* 7 vols., ed. Rolf Tiedemann and Hermann Schweppenhäuser, 3: 219–25. Frankfurt am Main: Suhrkamp, 1972–99.

————. *Einbahnstraße.* In *Gesammelte Schriften,* 7 vols., ed. Rolf Tiedemann and Hermann Schweppenhäuser, 4: 83–148. Frankfurt am Main: Suhrkamp, 1972–99.

————. "Ein Berliner Straßenjunge." In *Gesammelte Schriften,* 7 vols., ed. Rolf Tiedemann and Hermann Schweppenhäuser, 7: 92–98. Frankfurt am Main: Suhrkamp, 1972–99.

————. *Gesammelte Briefe.* Vols. 2–3. Ed. Henri Lonitz, Christoph Gödde. Theodor W. Adorno-Archiv. Frankfurt am Main: Suhrkamp, 1995–97.

————. *Goethes Wahlverwandtschaften.* In *Gesammelte Schriften,* 7 vols., ed. Rolf Tiedemann and Hermann Schweppenhäuser, 1: 123–201. Frankfurt am Main: Suhrkamp, 1972–99.

————. "Möbel und Masken." In *Gesammelte Schriften,* 7 vols., ed. Rolf Tiedemann and Hermann Schweppenhäuser, 4: 477–79. Frankfurt am Main: Suhrkamp, 1972–99.

————. "Moskau." In *Gesammelte Schriften,* 7 vols., ed. Rolf Tiedemann and Hermann Schweppenhäuser, 4: 316–48. Frankfurt am Main: Suhrkamp, 1972–99.

————. *The Origin of German Tragic Drama.* Trans. John Osborne. New York: Verso, 1998.

————. *Reflections: Essays, Aphorisms, Autobiographical Writings.* Trans. Edmund Jephcott. New York: Harcourt Brace Jovanovich, 1978.

————. Review of Jakob Job, *Neapel: Reisebilder und Skizzen.* In *Gesam-*

melte Schriften, 7 vols., ed. Rolf Tiedemann and Hermann Schweppenhäuser, 3: 132–35. Frankfurt am Main: Suhrkamp, 1972–99.

———. *Ursprung des deutschen Trauerspiels.* In *Gesammelte Schriften,* 7 vols., ed. Rolf Tiedemann and Hermann Schweppenhäuser, 1: 203–430. Frankfurt am Main: Suhrkamp, 1972–99.

———. "Zwei Gedichte von Friedrich Hölderlin. 'Dichtermut'—'Blödigkeit.'" In *Gesammelte Schriften,* 7 vols., ed. Rolf Tiedemann and Hermann Schweppenhäuser, 2: 105–26. Frankfurt am Main: Suhrkamp, 1972–99.

Benjamin, Walter, and Asja Lacis. "Neapel." In *Gesammelte Schriften,* 4: 307–16.

Bloch, Ernst. *Briefe, 1903–1975.* Vol. 1. Ed. Karola Bloch et al. Frankfurt am Main: Suhrkamp, 1985.

———. "Italien und die Porosität." In *Gesamtausgabe,* vol. 9, *Literarische Aufsätze,* pp. 508–15. Frankfurt am Main: Suhrkamp, 1965.

Blumenberg, Hans. *Schiffbruch mit Zuschauer: Paradigma einer Daseinsmetapher.* Frankfurt: Suhrkamp, 1997.

Bois-Reymond, Emil du, and Anton Dohrn. *Briefwechsel.* Ed. Christiane Groeben. Berlin: Springer, 1985.

Bolz, Nobert W., and Richard Faber. *Antike und Moderne: Zu Walter Benjamins "Passagen."* Würzburg: Königshausen + Neumann, 1986.

Bonss, Wolfgang. *Wie weiter mit Theodor W. Adorno?* Hamburg: Hamburger Edition, 2008.

Braunstein, Dirk. *Adornos Kritik der politischen Ökonomie.* Bielefeld: transcript, 2015.

Bredekamp, Horst. *Darwins Korallen: Frühe Evolutionsmodelle und die Tradition der Naturgeschichte.* Berlin: Wagenbach, 2005.

Brodersen, Momme. *Spinne im eigenen Netz: Walter Benjamin Leben und Werk.* Bühl-Moos: Elster, 1990.

Buck-Morss, Susan. *The Dialectics of Seeing: Walter Benjamin and the Arcades Project.* Cambridge, MA: MIT Press, 1991.

———. *The Origin of Negative Dialectics. Theodor W. Adorno, Walter Benjamin, and the Frankfurt Institute.* New York: Free Press, 1977.

Büchner, Georg. "Mémoire sur le système nerveux du Barbeau." *Mémoires de la Société du Museum d'Histoire Naturelle* 2 (1835): 1–57.

Cerio, Claretta. *Mein Capri.* Hamburg: Mare, 2010.

Cerio, Edwin. *Capri: Ein kleines Welttheater im Mittelmeer.* Trans. Nora Urban. Munich: Callwey, 1954.

Clavel, Gilbert. *Mein Bereich.* Basel: Schwabe, 1930.

Colli, Giorgio, and Mazzino Montinari, eds. *Briefe an Friedrich Nietzsche: Januar 1875—Dezember 1879.* Vol. 1. Berlin, New York: Walter de Gruyter, 1980.

Cook's Handbook to Naples and Environs. London: Cook, 1924.

Deleuze, Gilles, and Felix Guattari, "Introduction: Rhizome." In *A Thousand Plateaus,* vol. 2 of *Capitalism and Schizophrenia,* trans. Brian Massumi, pp. 3–25. Minneapolis: University of Minnesota Press, 1987.

Demirović, Alex. *Der nonkonformistische Intellektuelle: Die Entwicklung der Kritischen Theorie zur Frankfurter Schule.* Frankfurt am Main: Suhrkamp, 1999.

Derrida, Jacques. *Marx' Gespenster: Der Staat der Schuld, die Trauerarbeit und die neue Internationale.* Frankfurt am Main: Suhrkamp, 2004.

D'Iorio, Paolo. *Le voyage de Nietzsche à Sorrente: Genèse de la philosophie de l'esprit libre.* Paris: CNRS Éditions, 2012.

Douglas, Norman. *Looking Back: An Autobiographical Excursion.* New York: Harcourt, Brace, 1933.

Eisenstein, Sergei M. *Das dynamische Quadrat: Schriften zum Film.* Ed. Oksana Bulgakowa and Dietmar Hochmut. Leipzig: Reclam, 1988.

———. "Montage der Attraktionen." In *Das dynamische Quadrat: Schriften zum Film,* ed. Oksana Bulgakova and Dietmar Hochmuth, pp. 10–16. Leipzig: Reclam, 1988.

Enzensberger, Hans Magnus, "Eine Theorie des Tourismus." In *Einzelheiten I, Bewusstseinsindustrie,* pp. 179–205. Frankfurt am Main: Suhrkamp, 1967.

Fahlbusch, Markus. "Über Jazz." In *Schlüsseltexte der Kritischen Theorie,* ed. Axel Honneth et al., pp. 19–21. Wiesbaden: VS Verlag für Sozialwissenschaften, 2011.

Felsch, Philipp, and Martin Mittelmeier. "'Ich war ehrlich überrascht und erschrocken, wie umfangreich Sie geantwortet haben': Theodor W. Adorno korrespondiert mit seinen Lesern." *Kultur und Gespenster* 13 (2012): 159–99.

Fiorentino, Alessandro. *Memorie di Sorrento*. Naples: Electa Napoli, 1991.

Flaubert, Gustave. "Gustave Flaubert: Eleven Letters." Trans. Geoffrey Wall. *Cambridge Quarterly* 25, no. 3 (1996): 213–42.

Fontane, Theodor. *Werke, Schriften und Briefe*. Vol. 2. Ed. Walter Keitel and Helmuth Nürnberger. Munich: Hanser, 1979.

Frank, Manfred. "Stichworte zur Konstellationsforschung (aus Schleiermacherscher Inspiration)." In *Konstellationsforschung*, ed. Martin Mulsow and Marcelo Stamm, pp. 139–148. Frankfurt am Main: Suhrkamp, 2005.

Freytag, Carl. "Alfred Sohn-Rethel in Italien, 1924–1927." In Alfred Sohn-Rethel, *Das Ideal des Kaputten*, 2nd ed., pp. 39–52. Bremen: Wassmann, 1992.

———. "Die Sprache der Dinge: Alfred Sohn-Rethels 'Zwischenexistenz' in Positano (1924–1927)." In *Geld und Geltung: Zu Alfred Sohn-Rethels soziologischer Erkenntnistheorie*, ed. Rudolf Heinz and Jochen Hörisch, pp. 78–85. Würzburg: Königshausen & Neumann, 2006.

Friedlander, Eli. "The Measure of the Contingent: Walter Benjamin's Dialectical Image." *Boundary 2* 35, no. 3 (2008): 1–26.

Fritsch, Karl von. *Bericht über die Senckenbergische naturforschende Gesellschaft in Frankfurt am Main*. Frankfurt am Main: Ges., 1873.

Führer durch das Aquarium der Zoologischen Station zu Neapel. Naples: Francesco Giannini & Figli, 1925.

Gangl, Manfred. "Staatskapitalismus und Dialektik der Aufklärung." In *Jenseits Instrumenteller Vernunft: Kritische Studien zur "Dialektik der Aufklärung,"* ed. Manfred Gangl and Gérard Raulet, 158–86. Frankfurt am Main: Peter Lang, 1998.

Garber, Klaus. *Zum Bilde Walter Benjamins: Studien, Porträts, Kritiken*. Munich: Fink, 1992.

Gay, Peter. *The Bourgeois Experience: Victoria to Freud*. Vol. 1, *Education of the Senses*. New York: Oxford University Press, 1984.

Gilloch, Graeme. *Myth and Metropolis: Walter Benjamin and the City*. Malden, MA: Polity, 1996.

Goethe, Johann Wolfgang von. *Dichtung und Wahrheit*. In *Sämtliche Werke nach Epochen seines Schaffens*, 21 vols., ed. Karl Richter et al., vol. 16. Munich: Hanser, 1985–98.

———. *Die Wahlverwandtschaften*. In *Sämtliche Werke nach Epochen seines Schaffens,* 21 vols., ed. Karl Richter et al., 9: 283–529. Munich: Hanser, 1985–98.

———. *Italienische Reise*. In *Sämtliche Werke nach Epochen seines Schaffens,* 21 vols., ed. Karl Richter et al., vol. 15. Munich: Hanser, 1985–98.

Gregorovius, Ferdinand. *Wanderjahre in Italien*. Vol. 3. Leipzig: Brockhaus, 1865.

Groeben, Christiane. "Alfred Krupp, Anton Dohrn und Salvatore Lo Bianco: 'Pelagische Tiefseekampagnen um Capri, 1900–1902.'" In *Physische Anthropologie—Biologie des Menschen,* ed. Michael Kaasch et al., pp. 187–200. Berlin: VWB, 2007.

Grossheim, Michael. "Archaisches oder dialektisches Bild? Zum Kontext einer Debatte zwischen Adorno und Benjamin." *DVjS für Literaturwissenschaft und Geistesgeschichte* 71 (1997): 494–517.

Grotzinger, John, and Thomas Jordan. *Understanding Earth*. 7th ed. New York: W. H. Freeman, 2014.

Groys, Boris. "Die Stadt im Zeitalter ihrer touristischen Reproduzierbarkeit." In *Topologie der Kunst,* pp. 187–98. Munich: Hanser, 2003.

Gruner, Wolfgang. *Ein Schicksal, das ich mit sehr vielen anderen geteilt habe: Alfred Kantorowicz—sein Leben und seine Zeit von 1899 bis 1935*. Kassel: Kassel University Press, 2006.

Gumbrecht, Hans Ulrich. *In 1926: Living at the Edge of Time*. Cambridge, MA: Harvard University Press, 1997.

Gumnior, Helmut, and Rudolf Ringguth. *Horkheimer*. 6th ed. Reinbek bei Hamburg: Rowohlt, 1997.

Habermas, Jürgen. *Der philosophische Diskurs der Moderne*. Frankfurt am Main: Suhrkamp, 1988.

———. "The Entwinement of Myth and Enlightenment: Max Horkheimer and Theodor Adorno." In *The Philosophical Discourse of Modernity,* trans. Frederick G. Lawrence, pp. 106–30. Cambridge, MA: MIT Press, 1990.

Hagen, Wolfgang. "Davor hatte ich eine instinktive Abzirkelung." In *L'Invitation au Voyage—Zu Alfred Sohn-Rethel,* ed. Bettina Wassmann, pp. 1–12. Bremen: Wassmann, 1979.

Haselberg, Peter von. "Wiesengrund-Adorno." In *Theodor W. Adorno,* ed. Heinz Ludwig Arnold, 2nd ed., pp. 7–21. Munich: Edition Text & Kritik, 1983.

Hatzfeld, Adolf von. *Positano.* Freiburg: Pontos, 1925.

Hegel, Georg Wilhelm Friedrich. *Enzyklopädie der philosophischen Wissenschaften. Werke,* vol. 8. Frankfurt am Main: Suhrkamp, 1986.

———. *Phänomenologie des Geistes. Werke,* vol. 3. Frankfurt am Main: Suhrkamp, 1986.

Henrich, Dieter. *Grundlegung aus dem Ich: Untersuchungen zur Vorgeschichte des Idealismus.* Vol. 2. Frankfurt am Main: Suhrkamp, 2004.

Heuss, Theodor. *Anton Dohrn in Neapel.* Berlin: Atlantis, 1940.

Hillach, Ansgar. "Dialektisches Bild." In *Benjamins Begriffe,* ed. Michael Opitz and Erdmut Wizisla, 1: 186–229. Frankfurt am Main: Suhrkamp, 2000.

Hoffmann, Ludwig, and Dieter Wardetzky, eds. *Theateroktober: Beiträge zur Entwicklung des sowjetischen Theaters.* Frankfurt am Main: Röderberg, 1972.

Honneth, Axel. "Eine Physiognomie der kapitalistischen Lebensform: Skizze der Gesellschaftstheorie Adornos." In *Dialektik der Freiheit,* pp. 165–87. Frankfurt am Main: Suhrkamp, 2005.

———. "Gerechtigkeit im Vollzug. Adornos 'Einleitung' in die Negative Dialektik." In *Pathologien der Vernunft: Geschichte und Gegenwart der Kritischen Theorie,* pp. 93–111. Frankfurt am Main: Suhrkamp, 2007.

———. "Vorbemerkung." In *Dialektik der Freiheit,* ed. Axel Honneth, pp. 7–10. Frankfurt am Main: Suhrkamp, 2005.

Hörisch, Jochen. "Über die Sprache Adornos. Rundfunkgespräch mit Peter Kemper." In *Zeitschrift für Kritische Theorie* 18/19 (2004), pp. 264–81.

Horkheimer, Max. "Die gegenwärtige Lage der Sozialphilosophie und die Aufgaben eines Instituts für Sozialforschung." In *Gesammelte Schriften,* 19 vols., ed. Alfred Schmidt and Gunzelin Schmid Noerr, 3: 20–35. Frankfurt am Main: S. Fischer, 1985–96.

———. "Egoismus und Freiheitsbewegung." In *Gesammelte Schriften,* 19 vols., ed. Alfred Schmidt and Gunzelin Schmid Noerr, 4: 9–88. Frankfurt am Main: S. Fischer, 1985–96.

———. "L'île heureuse." In *Gesammelte Schriften,* 19 vols., ed. Alfred Schmidt and Gunzelin Schmid Noerr, 11: 289–328. Frankfurt am Main: S. Fischer, 1985–96.

Horkheimer, Max, and Theodor W. Adorno. *Dialectic of Enlightenment.* Ed. Gunzelin Schmid Noerr. Trans. Edmund Jephcott. Stanford, CA: Stanford University Press, 2002.

Hullot-Kentor, Robert. "Second Salvage: Prolegomenon to a Reconstruction of Current of Music" (editor's introduction). In *Current of Music: Elements of a Radio Theory,* by Theodor W. Adorno, ed. Robert Hullot-Kentor, pp. 1–40. Malden, MA: Polity, 2009.

Jäger, Lorenz. *Adorno: Eine politische Biographie.* Munich: Pantheon, 2009.

———. "Die esoterische Form." In *Europäische Barock-Rezeption,* ed. Klaus Garber, pp. 143–53. Wiesbaden: Harrassowitz, 1991.

———. *Die schöne Kunst, das Schicksal zu lesen: Kleines Brevier der Astrologie.* Springe: zu Klampen, 2009.

Jay, Martin. *Marxism and Totality.* Berkeley: University of California Press, 1984.

Jenemann, David. *Adorno in America.* Minneapolis: University of Minnesota Press, 2007.

Kafka, Franz. *Ein Landarzt und andere Drucke zu Lebzeiten.* Ed. Wolf Kittler, Hans-Gerd Koch, and Gerhard Neumann. 5th ed. Frankfurt am Main: S. Fischer, 2004.

Kant, Immanuel. *Kritik der Urteilskraft.* Hamburg: Meiner, 1990.

———. *Metaphysics of Morals.* Trans. Mary Gregor. Cambridge: Cambridge University Press, 1991.

Kantorowicz, Alfred. *Meine Kleider.* Berlin: Aufbau, 1957.

Kaulen, Heinrich. "Walter Benjamin und Asja Lacis: Eine biographische Konstellation und ihre Folgen." *DVjs* 69, no. 1 (1995): 92–122.

Kempter, Martina. "Nachwort." Afterword to Alberto Savinio, *Capri,* pp. 99–111. Frankfurt am Main: Insel, 2001.

Kesel, Humbert. *Capri: Biographie einer Insel.* Ansbach: Prestel, 1971.

Klee, Paul. *Briefe an die Familie, 1893–1940.* Ed. Felix Klee. Vol. 1. Cologne: Dumont, 1979.

———. *Tagebücher, 1898–1918.* Ed. Paul-Klee-Stiftung. Stuttgart: Hatje, 1988.

Klein, Richard, Johann Kreuzer, and Stefan Müller-Doohm, eds. *Adorno-Handbuch.* Stuttgart: Metzler, 2011.

Kleinwort, Malte. "Zur Desorientierung im Manuskript der Vorrede zu Benjamins Trauerspielbuch." In *Benjamin-Studien* 2, ed. Daniel Weidner and Sigrid Weigel (2011): 87–110.

Kluge, Alexander. *Nachrichten aus der ideologischen Antike* (3 DVDs). Frankfurt am Main: Suhrkamp, 2008.

Kolesch, Doris. *Das Schreiben des Subjekts: Zur Inszenierung ästhetischer Subjektivität bei Baudelaire, Barthes und Adorno*. Vienna: Passagen, 1996.

Kopisch, August. *Die Entdeckung der Blauen Grotte auf der Insel Capri*. Ed. Dieter Richter. Berlin: Wagenbach, 1997.

Kracauer, Siegfried. "Das Ornament der Masse." In *Werke*, ed. Inka Mülder-Bach et al., 5.2: 612–24. Frankfurt am Main: Suhrkamp, 2004–11.

———. "Der Detektiv-Roman: Eine Deutung." In *Werke*, ed. Inka Mülder-Bach et al., 1: 103–209. Frankfurt am Main: Suhrkamp, 2004–11.

———. "Der verbotene Blick." In *Werke*, ed. Inka Mülder-Bach et al., 5.2: 224–27. Frankfurt am Main: Suhrkamp, 2004–11.

———. "Die Angestellten. Aus dem neuesten Deutschland." In *Werke*, ed. Inka Mülder-Bach et al., 1: 211–310. Frankfurt am Main: Suhrkamp, 2004–11.

———. "Die Bibel auf Deutsch." In *Werke*, ed. Inka Mülder-Bach et al., 5.2: 374–86. Frankfurt am Main: Suhrkamp, 2004–11.

———. "Die Reise und der Tanz." In *Werke*, ed. Inka Mülder-Bach et al., 5.2: 214–23. Frankfurt am Main: Suhrkamp, 2004–11.

———. "Die Wartenden." In *Werke*, ed. Inka Mülder-Bach et al., 5.1: 383–94. Frankfurt am Main: Suhrkamp, 2004–11.

———. "Felsenwahn in Positano." In *Werke*, ed. Inka Mülder-Bach et al., 5.2: 296–303. Frankfurt am Main: Suhrkamp, 2004–11.

———. *Georg*. In *Werke*, ed. Inka Mülder-Bach et al., 7: 257–516. Frankfurt am Main: Suhrkamp, 2004–11.

———. "Gestalt und Zerfall." In *Werke*, ed. Inka Mülder-Bach et al., 5.2 283–88. Frankfurt am Main: Suhrkamp, 2004–11.

———. *Ginster*. In *Werke*, ed. Inka Mülder-Bach et al., 7: 9–256. Frankfurt am Main: Suhrkamp, 2004–11.

———. "Kult der Zerstreuung." In *Werke*, ed. Inka Mülder-Bach et al., 6.1: 208–13. Frankfurt am Main: Suhrkamp, 2004–11.

———. "Langeweile." In *Werke,* ed. Inka Mülder-Bach et al., 5.2: 161–64. Frankfurt am Main: Suhrkamp, 2004–11.

———. "Lichtreklame." In *Werke,* ed. Inka Mülder-Bach et al., 5.2: 529–32. Frankfurt am Main: Suhrkamp, 2004–11.

———. *The Mass Ornament.* Trans. Thomas Y. Levin. Cambridge, MA: Harvard University Press, 1995.

———. Review of Adolf von Hatzfeld, *Positano.* In *Frankfurter Zeitung,* February 7, 1926, p. 6.

———. "Zu Sorrent." In *Werke,* ed. Inka Mülder-Bach et al., 5.2: 339–40. Frankfurt am Main: Suhrkamp, 2004–11.

La Capria, Raffaele. "Neapel als geistige Landschaft." In *Neapel: Eine literarische Einladung,* ed. Dieter Richter, pp. 7–17. Berlin: Wagenbach, 1988.

Lacis, Asja. *Revolutionär im Beruf: Berichte über proletarisches Theater, über Meyerhold, Brecht, Benjamin und Piscator.* Ed. Hildegard Brenner. Munich: Rogner & Bernhard, 1971.

Leitfaden für das Aquarium der Zoologischen Station zu Neapel. 6th ed. Naples: Trani, 1905.

Lenhard, Philipp. *Friedrich Pollock: Die graue Eminenz der Frankfurter Schule.* Frankfurt am Main: Suhrkamp, 2019.

Lévi-Strauss, Claude. *Wild Thought.* Trans. Jeffrey Mehlman and John Leavitt. Chicago: University of Chicago Press, 2021.

Lo Bianco, Salvatore, "Metodi usati nella Stazione zoologica per la conservazione degli animali marini." *Mittheilungen aus der Zoologischen Station zu Neapel* 9 (1890): 434–74.

———. *Pelagische Tiefseefischerei der "Maja" in der Umgebung von Capri.* Jena: Gustav Fischer, 1904.

Löwenthal, Leo, and Siegfried Kracauer. *In steter Freundschaft: Briefwechsel,* ed. Peter-Erwin Jansen and Christian Schmidt. Springe: zu Klampen, 2003.

Lukács, Georg. *Die Theorie des Romans.* Berlin: Cassirer, 1920.

———. *Geschichte und Klassenbewusstsein.* Darmstadt: Luchterhand, 1968.

———. *History and Class Consciousness.* Trans. Rodney Livingstone. Cambridge, MA: MIT Press, 1972.

————. *The Theory of the Novel*. Trans. Anna Bostock. Cambridge, MA: MIT Press, 1971.

Maak, Niklas. *Der Architekt am Strand: Le Corbusier und das Geheimnis der Seeschnecke*. Munich: Hanser, 2010.

Machatschek, Michael. *Golf von Neapel*. Erlangen: Müller, 2011.

Malaparte, Curzio. *The Skin*. Trans. David Moore. New York: New York Review of Books, 2013.

Mann, Thomas. *Der Zauberberg*. Ed. Michael Neumann. *Große Kommentierte Frankfurter Ausgabe*, ed. Heinrich Detering et al., vol. 5.1. Frankfurt am Main: S. Fischer, 2002.

————. *Doktor Faustus*. Ed. Ruprecht Wimmer. *Große Kommentierte Frankfurter Ausgabe*, ed. Heinrich Detering et al., vol. 10. Frankfurt am Main: S. Fischer, 2007.

————. *Doktor Faustus*. Commentary by Ruprecht Wimmer. *Große Kommentierte Frankfurter Ausgabe*, ed. Heinrich Detering et al., vol. 10. Frankfurt am Main: S. Fischer, 2007.

Marx, Karl. *Capital: A Critique of Political Economy*. Vol. 1 of 3. Trans. Ben Fowkes and Ernest Mandel. New York: Penguin Books, 1992.

————. *Das Kapital*. In *Marx-Engels-Werke*, 44 vols., ed. Institut für Marxismus-Leninismus beim Zentralkomitee der SED, vol. 23. Berlin: Dietz, 1968.

————. *Der achtzehnte Brumaire des Louis Bonaparte*. In *Marx-Engels-Werke*, 44 vols., ed. Institut für Marxismus-Leninismus beim Zentralkomitee der SED, vol. 8. Berlin: Dietz, 1972.

McGill, Justine. "The Porous Coupling of Walter Benjamin and Asja Lacis." *Angelaki* 13, no. 2 (2008): 59–72.

Menninghaus, Winfried. "Das Ausdruckslose: Walter Benjamins Kritik des Schönen durch das Erhabene." In *Walter Benjamin, 1892–1940 zum 100. Geburtstag*, ed. Uwe Steiner, pp. 33–76. Bern: Peter Lang, 1992.

————. "Kant, Hegel und Marx in Lukács' Theorie der Verdinglichung: Destruktion eines neomarxistischen 'Klassikers.'" In *Spiegel und Gleichnis: Festschrift für Jacob Taubes*, ed. Norbert W. Bolz and Wolfgang Hübener, pp. 318–30. Würzburg: Königshausen & Neumann, 1983.

————. *Unendliche Verdopplung: Die frühromantische Grundlegung der Kunsttheorie im Begriff absoluter Selbstreflexion*. Frankfurt am Main: Suhrkamp, 1987.

————. *Walter Benjamins Theorie der Sprachmagie*. Frankfurt am Main: Suhrkamp, 1995.

Mittelmeier, Martin. "Es gibt kein richtiges Sich-Ausstrecken in der falschen Badewanne: Wie Adornos berühmtester Satz wirklich lautet—ein Gang ins Archiv." *Recherche* 4 (2009): 3.

Money, James. *Capri: Island of Pleasure*. London: Hamilton, 1986.

Morgenstern, Soma. *Alban Berg und seine Idole: Erinnerungen und Briefe*. Berlin: Aufbau, 1999.

Mosebach, Martin. *Die schöne Gewohnheit zu leben: Eine italienische Reise*. Berlin: Berlin Verlag, 1997.

Mosès, Stéphan. Der *Engel der Geschichte: Franz Rosenzweig, Walter Benjamin, Gershom Scholem*. Frankfurt am Main: Jüdischer, 1994.

Müller, Tobi. "Karl Marx und die gespenstische Gallerte." In *Tages-Anzeiger* 47 (2007): 47.

Müller-Doohm, Stefan. *Adorno: Eine Biographie*. Frankfurt am Main: Suhrkamp, 2003.

Müller-Sievers, Helmut. *Desorientierung: Anatomie und Dichtung bei Georg Büchner*. Göttingen: Wallstein, 2003.

Munthe, Axel. *Das Buch von San Michele*. Trans. G. Uexküll-Schwerin. Munich: dtv, 1978.

————. *The Story of San Michele: Autobiography of a Swedish Doctor*. London: Murray, 1929.

Neapel und Umgebung. Griebens Reiseführer, vol. 101. Berlin: Verlag von Griebens Reiseführern, 1925.

Nietzsche, Friedrich. *Digitale Kritische Gesamtausgabe*. Ed. Paolo D'Iorio. Digital version of Friedrich Nietzsche, *Werke: Kritische Gesamtausgabe*. Ed. Giorgio Colli and Mazzino Montinari. Berlin, New York: de Gruyter, 1967–.

Norton, Leslie. *Leonide Massine and the 20th Century Ballet*. Jefferson, NC: McFarland, 2004.

Pabst, Reinhard. *Kindheit in Amorbach*. Frankfurt am Main: Insel, 2003.

Palmier, Jean-Michel. *Walter Benjamin: Lumpensammler, Engel und buck-licht Männlein; Ästhetik und Politik bei Walter Benjamin.* Frankfurt am Main: Suhrkamp, 2009.

Paškevica, Beata. *In der Stadt der Parolen: Asja Lacis, Walter Benjamin und Bertolt Brecht.* Essen: Klartext, 2006.

Pisani, Salvatore. "Baustoffe." In *Neapel: Sechs Jahrhunderte Kulturgeschichte,* ed. Salvatore Pisani and Katharina Siebenmorgen, pp. 214–21. Berlin: Reimer, 2009.

———. "Neapel-Topoi." In *Neapel: Sechs Jahrhunderte Kulturgeschichte,* ed. Salvatore Pisani and Katharina Siebenmorgen, pp. 28–37. Berlin: Reimer, 2009.

Platen, August von. *Die Tagebücher des Grafen August von Platen: Aus der Handschrift des Dichters.* Vol. 2. Stuttgart: Cotta, 1900.

Platthaus, Isabel. *Höllenfahrten: Die epische katabis und die Unterwelten der Moderne.* Munich: Wilhelm Fink Verlag, 2004.

Reich, Bernhard. "Erinnerungen an das frühe sowjetische Theater." In *Theateroktober: Beiträge zur Entwicklung des sowjetischen Theaters,* ed. Ludwig Hoffmann and Dieter Wardetzky, pp. 7–31. Frankfurt am Main: Röderberg, 1972.

———. *Im Wettlauf mit der Zeit.* Berlin: Henschel, 1970.

Reijen, Willem van, and Jan Bransen. "Das Verschwinden der Klassengeschichte in der 'Dialektik der Aufklärung': Ein Kommentar zu den Textvarianten der Buchausgabe von 1947 gegenüber der Erstveröffentlichung von 1944." In Max Horkheimer, *Gesammelte Schriften,* 19 vols., ed. Alfred Schmidt and Gunzelin Schmid Noerr, 5: 453–57. Frankfurt am Main: S. Fischer, 1987.

Richter, Dieter. "Bruder Glücklichs trauriges Ende." *Die Zeit* 31 (2002): 74.

———. "Das blaue Feuer der Romantik, Geschichte und Mythos der Blauen Grotte." In August Kopisch, *Die Entdeckung der Blauen Grotte auf der Insel Capri,* ed. Dieter Richter, pp. 61–107. Berlin: Wagenbach, 1997.

———. *Der Vesuv: Geschichte eines Berges.* 2nd ed. Berlin: Wagenbach, 2007.

———. "Friedrich Alfred Krupp auf Capri: Ein Skandal und seine Geschichte." In *Friedrich Alfred Krupp. Ein Unternehmer im Kaiserreich,* ed. Michael Epkenhans and Ralf Stremmel, pp. 157–77. Munich: C. H. Beck, 2010.

———. *Neapel: Biographie einer Stadt*. Berlin: Wagenbach, 2005.

Richter, Gerhard. "Die Erbschaft der Konstellation: Adorno und Hegel." *MLN* 126 (2011): 446–70.

Roth, Udo. *Georg Büchners naturwissenschaftliche Schriften*. Tübingen: Niemeyer, 2004.

Savinio, Alberto. *Capri*. Trans. John Shepley. Marlboro, VT: Marlboro Press, 1989.

Schiemenz, P. Review of Salvatore Lo Bianco's *Metodi usati nella Stazione zoologica per la conservazione degli animali marini*. *Zeitschrift für wissenschaftliche Mikroskopie und für mikroskopische Technik* 8 (1891): 54–66.

Schlüter, Andreas, ed. *Der Golf von Neapel: Ein Reiselesebuch*. Hamburg: Ellert & Richter, 2009.

Schmitt, Thomas, and Thomas Steinfeld. *Exil, Eden, Endstation: Die Luftschlösser von Capri*. Tag/Traum Filmproduktion, WDR/arte, 2004. 52 mins.

Schnebel, Dieter. "Komposition von Sprache—sprachliche Gestaltung von Musik in Adornos Werk." In *Theodor W. Adorno zum Gedächtnis*, ed. Hermann Schweppenhäuser, pp. 129–43. Frankfurt am Main: Suhrkamp, 1971.

Schöttker, Detlev. *Konstruktiver Fragmentarismus: Form und Rezeption der Schriften Walter Benjamins*. Frankfurt am Main: Suhrkamp, 1999.

Schwanhäußer, Anja. *Kosmonauten des Underground: Ethnografie einer Berliner Szene*. Frankfurt am Main: Campus, 2010.

Smith, Paul. "Thomas Cook & Son's Vesuvius Railway." In *Japan Railway and Transport Review* 3 (1998): 10–15.

Sohn-Rethel, Alfred. "Aus einem Gespräch von Alfred Sohn-Rethel mit Uwe Herms über 'Geistige und Körperliche Arbeit' 1973." In *L'invitation au voyage—zu Alfred Sohn-Rethel,* ed. Bettina Wassmann. Bremen: Wassmann, 1979, pp. 1–16.

———. "Das Ideal des Kaputten: Über neapolitanische Technik." In *Das Ideal des Kaputten,* ed. Carl Freytag, pp. 33–38. Bremen: Wassmann, 1992.

—. "Eine Verkehrsstockung in der Via Chiaia." In *Das Ideal des Kaputten,* ed. Carl Freytag, pp. 7–19. Bremen: Wassmann, 1992.

—. "Einige Unterbrechungen waren wirklich unnötig." In *Die Zerstörung einer Zukunft. Gespräche mit emigrierten Sozialwissenschaftlern,* recorded by Matthias Greffrath. Reinbek bei Hamburg: Rowohlt, 1979.

—. *Erinnerungen.* Transcript of a three-hour radio portrait of Wolfgang Hagen for Radio Bremen in 1977. Available at Wayback Machine, http://web.archive.org/web/20050426112218fw_/http://www.radiobremen.de/online/sohn_rethel/erinner/index.htm (accessed January 24, 2024).

—. "Exposee zum theoretischen Kommentar der Marxschen Gesellschaftslehre." Bundesarchiv, Koblenz, M 1492,26.

—. *Geistige und körperliche Arbeit: Zur Epistemologie der abendländischen Geschichte.* Frankfurt am Main: Suhrkamp, 1970.

—. "Kommentar zum 'Exposé zum theoretischen Kommentar der Marxschen Gesellschaftslehre' von 1926." In *Von der Analytik des Wirtschaftens zur Theorie der Volkswirtschaft: Frühe Schriften,* ed. Oliver Schlaudt and Carl Freytag, pp. 153–55. Freiburg: ça ira, 2012.

—. *Soziologische Theorie der Erkenntnis.* Frankfurt am Main: Suhrkamp, 1985.

—. "Vesuvbesteigung 1926." In *Das Ideal des Kaputten,* ed. Carl Freytag, pp. 21–31. Bremen: Wassmann, 1992.

Sonnentag, Stefanie. *Spaziergänge durch das literarische Capri und Neapel.* Zurich: Arche, 2003.

Spina, Luigi. "Der Mythos der Sirene Parthenope." In *Neapel: Sechs Jahrhunderte Kulturgeschichte,* ed. Salvatore Pisani and Katharina Siebenmorgen, pp. 23–27. Berlin: Reimer, 2009.

Stamm, Marcelo. "Konstellationsforschung—Ein Methodenprofil: Motive und Perspektiven." In *Konstellationsforschung,* ed. Martin Mulsow and Marcelo Stamm, pp. 31–73. Frankfurt am Main: Suhrkamp, 2005.

Steinert, Heinz. *Adorno in Wien: Über die (Un)Möglichkeit von Kunst, Kultur und Befreiung.* Vienna: Verlag für Gesellschaftskritik, 1989.

Steinfeld, Thomas. *Der Arzt von San Michele: Axel Munthe und die Kunst, dem Leben einen Sinn zu geben.* Munich: Hanser, 2007.

Striedter, Jurij. "Zur formalistischen Theorie der Prosa und der litera-rischen Evolution." In *Russischer Formalismus: Texte zur allgemeinen Literaturtheorie und zur Theorie der Prosa,* ed. Jurij Striedter, pp. ix–lxxxiii. Munich: Fink, 1969.

Szeemann, Harald. "Gilbert Clavel, 1883–1927. Sein Lebensgang in Brie-fen." In *Visionäre Schweiz,* ed. Harald Szeemann, pp. 234–96. Aarau: Sauerländer, 1991.

Szondi, Peter. "Benjamins Städtebilder." In *Lektüren und Lektionen,* pp. 134–49. Frankfurt am Main: Suhrkamp, 1973.

Theodor W. Adorno Archiv, ed. "Adornos Seminar vom Sommersemes-ter 1932 über Benjamins *Ursprung des deutschen Trauerspiels.* Proto-kolle." In *Frankfurter Adorno Blätter IV,* ed. Theodor W. Adorno Ar-chiv, pp. 52–77. Munich: Edition Text + Kritik, 1995.

Tiedemann, Rolf. "Begriff, Bild, Name: Über Adornos Utopie der Er-kenntnis." In *Frankfurter Adorno Blätter II,* ed. Theodor W. Adorno Archiv, pp. 92–111. Munich: Edition Text + Kritik, 1993.

Vennen, Mareike. *Medialisierungen des Lebendigen—Das Aquarium zwi-schen Natur und Technik von 1840 bis 1930.* Unpublished, n.d.

Voss, Julia. *Darwins Bilder: Ansichten der Evolutionstheorie, 1837–1874.* Frankfurt: S. Fischer, 2007.

Wagner, Horst-Günter. *Die Kulturlandschaft am Vesuv: Eine agrargeogra-phische Strukturanalyse mit Berücksichtigung der jungen Wandlungen.* Hanover: Selbstverlag der Geographischen Gesellschaft, 1967.

Walter Benjamin Archiv, ed. *Bilder, Texte und Zeichen.* Frankfurt am Main: Suhrkamp, 2006.

Wellmer, Albrecht. "Wahrheit, Schein, Versöhnung: Adornos ästheti-sche Rettung der Modernität," In *Zur Dialektik von Moderne und Post-moderne: Vernunftkritik nach Adorno,* pp. 9–47. Frankfurt am Main: Suhrkamp, 1985.

Wiggershaus, Rolf. *Die Frankfurter Schule: Geschichte, theoretische Ent-wicklung, politische Bedeutung.* 2nd ed. Munich: dtv, 1989.

———. "Friedrich Pollock—der letzte Unbekannte der Frankfurter Schule." *Die Neue Gesellschaft: Frankfurter Hefte* 8 (1994): 750–56.

Ziege, Eva-Maria. *Antisemitismus und Gesellschaftstheorie: Die Frankfurter Schule im amerikanischen Exil.* Frankfurt am Main: Suhrkamp, 2009.

Acknowledgments

Winfried Menninghaus, without whose delightfully subversive approach this way of reading Adorno would not exist.

Anja Schwanhäußer for the many discussions, the critical, and the inspiring preliminary proofreading.

Philipp Felsch for submitting to intense interrogations about Adorno and for academic guidance.

Thomas Rathnow for the trust, Tobias Winstel for the courage and the enthusiastic accompaniment. Antje Korsmeier for precise and insightful editing. Michael Gaeb for the excitement in matters of theory and for encouraging me to take up the text once again. Michael Schwarz and Ursula Marx at the Adorno and Benjamin Archives for their tremendous helpfulness and their many valuable pointers. Christiane Groeben for a wonderful afternoon at one of the world's most beautiful workplaces and for finding the calling cards. Bettina Wassmann and Oliver Schlaudt for their assistance with the Sohn-Rethel estate.

Shelley Frisch, for the magnificent linguistic rendering.

Charlotte M. Craig Visiting Research Scholar and the Max Kade Writer/Scholar in Residence Program in the Department of German at Rutgers University (New Brunswick), which enabled me to revise and update the text.

MARTIN MITTELMEIER (1971) is Honorary Professor at the Institute for German Language and Literature at the University of Cologne. After having worked for many years as an editor at several German publishing houses, he now lives and works in Cologne as a freelance editor and author. He has published several works on German intellectual history, including *Dada: A Century's Tale* (2016) and *Freedom and Darkness* (2021).

SHELLEY FRISCH is a translator from German, best known for her translations of biographies of Franz Kafka, Friedrich Nietzsche, Albert Einstein, and Leonardo da Vinci. Her translations have won the Helen and Kurt Wolff Translation Prize and the Aldo and Jeanne Scaglione Translation Prize; and have been long-listed for the National Translation Award, the National Book Critics Circle Award, and the PEN Translation Prize. She holds a PhD in German from Princeton University.